# THINKING FUTURES

Derrick Gosselin | Bruno Tindemans

# Thinking Futures

*Strategy at the Edge
of Complexity and Uncertainty*

Cover image:  An astrolabe made by the astronomer Abu Bakr ibn Yusuf in the year 1216 AD or 613 AH
in the city of Marrakesh. Museum Paul Dupuy, Toulouse, France.
Photo: © 2002, Nicolas Brodu.

This book is an extended, updated and adapted translation of *Toekomstmakers. Hoe besturen bij onzekerheid*, LannooCampus Publishers (2012).

D/2016/45/135 – ISBN 978 94 014 2668 8 – NUR 801, 805

Cover design: Compagnie Paul Verrept
Interior design: 5NUL8 Grafische Producties

© Derrick Gosselin, Bruno Tindemans & Lannoo Publishers nv, Tielt, 2016.

LannooCampus Publishers is a subsidiary of Lannoo Publishers, the book and multimedia division of Lannoo Publishers nv.

LannooCampus Publishers
Erasme Ruelensvest 179 box 101
3001 Leuven
Belgium
www.lannoocampus.com

# Astrolabe

The cover image presents an astrolabe made by the astronomer Abu Bakr ibn Yusuf in the year 1216 AD in the city of Marrakesh.

The astrolabe is an ancient astronomical computer for solving problems in such diverse areas as astronomy, astrology, navigation, surveying and timekeeping. Its name is derived from the Greek word *astrolabos* (ἀστρολάβος), a combination of '*astron*' meaning 'star' and '*lambanein*' meaning 'to take'. The Oxford English Dictionary translates 'astrolabe' as 'star-taker', since it takes measurements of the positions of stars. More than two thousand years ago, the Greek astronomer Hipparchus of Nicaea (c.190 – c. 120 BC) already knew the principles of the astrolabe and by the year 800 the Islamic world had already developed numerous sophisticated applications. Its use was introduced to Europe from Muslim Spain (Al-Andalus) in the early 12$^{th}$ century. In Europe, the astrolabe became the most important tool for astronomers until the middle of the 17$^{th}$ century, while in the Arab world its use continued until the 19$^{th}$ century.

The 18$^{th}$ century Radcliffe Observatory of Green Templeton College in Oxford was among the first modern scientific observatories in the world. Its construction was inspired by the *Tower of the Winds* in the Roman Agora in Athens. Today, the University of Oxford still possesses one of the largest collections of astrolabes in the world, conserved at its Museum of the History of Science.

Astrolabes are outstanding scientific instruments for the solution of complex problems relating to the *navigation of unchartered territory*, while its crafting and use requires a vast multi-disciplinary knowledge. Consequently, astrolabes have many things in common with complexity theory and futures research, but also with Green Templeton, the Oxford Martin School and the University of Oxford.

**THINKING**: the act of producing thoughts or the process of producing thoughts. Thinking allows humans to solve problems, to make sense of, interpret, represent or model the world they experience, and also to make predictions about that world. It is therefore helpful to an organism with needs, objectives and desires, as it makes plans or otherwise attempts to accomplish those goals.

**FUTURE**: after the time right now; the time after the current time; the next time; an action or condition that has not yet happened; an undefined moment in time that still needs to take place; a situation of someone or something at a later date.

**STRATEGY**: from the Greek word *stratēgia* (στρατηγία) meaning 'generalship'; based on the word *stratēgos* (στραταγός) meaning 'army leader', which is a combination of *stratos* meaning 'army' and *agein* meaning 'to lead'. A plan of action designed to achieve a long-term or overall aim.

**STRATEGIC** – important or essential in relation to a plan of action; highly important to or an integral part of a strategy or plan of action; highly important to an intended objective.

**COMPLEXITY**: something complex. **COMPLEX** – difficult to understand for being intricate or involved; complicated.

**UNCERTAINTY**: the state of being uncertain. **UNCERTAIN** – not able to be relied on; not known or definite; not completely confident or sure of something.

**SCENARIO**: plausible, coherent stories about the future aimed at making sense of uncertain issues and clarifying strategic options for decision-makers. Scenarios provide a non-threatening environment for exploring multiple perspectives, creating a shared language and leading to understanding and trust.

Announcer; Augur; Futurism; Futurology; Chance; Tomorrow; Opportunity; Oracle; Perspective; Prediction; Prophet; Prophetic; Prophecies; Prophesy; Prognosis; Scenario; Scenario-based thinking; Scenario learning; Scenario planning; Scenario studies; Science fiction; Future; Future scanning; Future image; Future thinking, Future planning; Future projection; Future engineering; Future research; Future scenario; Future expectation; Future event; Promulgator; Perspective; Horizon; Expectation; Vision; Visionary; Predict; Predictor; Prospect; Look ahead; Prompter; Anticipate; Astrologer; Seer.

To
Anne-France and Marie-Charlotte Gosselin
D.P.G.


For
Matthias, Hannah, and Andreas Tindemans
B.T.

# Contents

# Figures

# Tables

# Prologue

*One evening in the autumn of 2000, Professor David Anthony King FRS entered his office in the Department of Trade and Industry in Whitehall, central London, little knowing what catastrophic document was destined to land on his desk in the near future.*

*It was October 2000, and King had just been appointed as Chief Scientific Advisor to Her Majesty's Government and Head of the Government Office for Science for the United Kingdom. This was a prestigious function with far reaching powers, since he reported directly to the Prime Minister and the Cabinet. In this function he was able to work on a more scientific approach for the great challenges facing the country. There was great hope that he could overcome the unavoidable daily political bickering and present an agenda based on science and studies.*

*David King is a top scientist at the chemistry department of the University of Cambridge and this new task suited him perfectly: organizing a scientific basis for economic policy in the broad sense of the word.*

*But the file that ended up on his desk a few weeks later would make him doubt his faith in this approach. The problem was gigantic: a local outbreak of foot-and-mouth disease threatened to become a major epidemic. David King had the opportunity to demonstrate his new approach. He summoned his colleagues and gave them instructions: firstly, they had to systematically follow up and map out the facts; next, they had to collect data of previous comparable crises; finally, they needed to determine the possible impact. All of this information would then form the basis of a well-founded approach that would be in proportion to the possible scale of contamination and damage.*

*So much for the theory; in practice, however, it was completely different. Not only were there constant reports of new outbreaks of the disease at new sites but there was an even worse conclusion that could no longer be avoided: there was no system to map out the possible contamination. To make matters worse, the available facts about previous crises were inadequate. This crisis was fundamentally different from any other. Even the expertise of academic experts in computer models for epidemics could not provide the necessary answers. They felt constantly one step behind events, and the crisis gradually assumed unknown proportions, with international consequences and huge economic loss for the farmers.*

**Al Gore (l) – Sir David King (r).**
**7 July 2009 – Inaugural World Forum on Enterprise and the Environment.**

Professor King, founding director of the *Smith School of Enterprise and the Environment*[1] at the University of Oxford, looked back on this turbulent period during a workshop at the end of 2009.

> "It was hell. I swore I never want to go through this again. The situation changed every day. The speed at which the epidemic spread had never been seen before. Data and models from the past were insufficient. This was a new situation. Models based on historical data were as good as worthless because there were too many new uncertainties. The complexity got continuously bigger and we were unable to propose well-founded measures. In short, I had nothing to base this serious policy on."

Methods and techniques from the past were inadequate for such new and unseen challenges. Better methods needed to be found in order to solve these *wicked problems*. And that is the focus of this book: the need for a new approach and the necessity to implement that approach as a decision-making process. As we shall see, this is not only relevant for problems relating to the health of British livestock.

# Chapter 1
# Thinking about the unthinkable

*"In order to be able to draw a limit to thought, we should first have to find both sides of the limit of what is thinkable (i.e. we should have to be able to think what cannot be thought)."*[2]

Ludwig J. Wittgenstein (1889-1951)

$$e^{i\pi} + 1 = 0$$

Leonard Euler (1707-1783)[3]

## Introduction

The 21st century started with a number of major changes. The financial crisis was not the only wake-up call. Many challenges of an unprecedented global scale have been sent to try us. The shift of economic activity to new growth countries, the pandemic proportions of ailments in humans and animals, the ageing population, migration flows, climate change, the meteoric technological evolutions and the scarcity of raw materials, energy and water – to name only a few – will cause shocks that will provide both new challenges and new opportunities. A stable environment seems to be a thing of the past. Our new environment has three distinct attributes that will increase as time progresses: rate of change, uncertainty, and complexity.

The analyses, the instruments and the methods that were used in the past to prepare for the future no longer work in this new context.[4]

Moreover, the promise of the information society is not being fulfilled. While the economic and political players accept and apply the latest news and the most recent data, the current crisis shows that the information available remains inadequate. It is inadequate to understand what is going on, inadequate to protect what exists and inadequate to create a better future.

The key lies in the correct interpretation or *sensemaking*[5] of the changes, in understanding and being able to place the events in this new environment. It also lies in the interpretation of *weak signals* that can help to understand what is coming up and so better prepare for the future. However, the key lies neither in the quantity nor in the speed with which information is available.

We must learn to observe, watch, interpret and understand, again.

Preparing the future in such an environment requires a different and new approach. In short, as the experience of Sir David illustrated, extrapolations of what has worked in the past and models that depart from a stable environment are no longer sufficient.

This book aims to give the reader insight into a new approach, a new way of future thinking. This is a powerful and academically based method to interpret an unpredictable, changing and complex environment. The term *future thinking* is used for a collection of methods, such as scenario-based thinking, new leadership and strategic conversation. We will see that the application domain is wide, ranging from political policy and business strategy to innovation and entrepreneurship. In all these domains, the disciplined application of future thinking can offer a competitive advantage in each new environment.

Scenario-based thinking is – in a nutshell – an approach that sharpens the skill to develop alternative futures and to test the current model of an organization. This approach brings hidden premises from the past to the surface and highlights them with alternative assumptions. The approach is used to anticipate future uncertainties. It offers a powerful method to proactively identify opportunities and to create – in the form of a new policy orientation – the renewal of an organization to adapt to its environment, a better strategic approach, or the conquest of new markets with new creative combinations. This approach is not limited by implicit and explicit assumptions from past hypotheses, which all too often turn out to be a dominant factor in the downfall of successful organizations.

In addition, 'future thinking' offers the instruments to discover the relationships between different and, at first glance, seemingly unconnected elements. It bridges the boundaries between experts, strategists and practitioners; in short, between all the relevant stakeholders. In this way, the knowledge of all these actors can be shared in a productive way to accelerate implementation when there is change. This makes it possible to anticipate an uncertain future with greater accuracy.

It is the best and perhaps the only reliable way to create a new model of leadership in each new environment and to discuss the unthinkable in order to resolve conflicts. We will discuss this in more depth later in the book. First, we will look at the origin of 'future thinking': where does it come from?

## History

### The origins of future thinking

Throughout history, people in leading, controlling or commanding positions have always shown keen interest in obtaining knowledge about the future. The biblical kings had their prophets, the Persian sultans their viziers, the Greek city-states their oracles, the Romans their divines, the Renaissance kings their astrologers and modern captains of industry their consultants and (sometimes) investment bankers. Even the Mafia has its *consiglieri*!

The first writings that attempted to define alternative futures were a form of essay that either described a place where everything was as bad as possible (*dystopia*) or, on the contrary, where everything was as good as possible (*utopia*): a perfectly happy state of being, such as Plato's ideal state in his *Politeia*.

The origin of strategic scenario-based thinking as a strategic planning tool is to be found in the military sciences. Early examples of the military use of scenario-based thinking usually took the form of simulations or war games. The modern approach to handling uncertainty through the use of different alternatives – today we would call these 'scenarios' – was first documented as being employed by German military strategists. The 19th century writings of General Carl von Clausewitz[6] (1780-1831) and General Helmuth von Moltke[7] the Younger (1848-1916), two Prussian military strategists to whom the first formulation of the principles of strategic planning is attributed, reveal that scenarios were used to present a broad range of future eventualities to support strategic decision-making.

Modern 'strategic scenario-based thinking' or 'scenario planning' as known and applied today, only emerged only after the Second World War. Its origins date back to the early 1950s and it evolved simultaneously in two separate geographic centres: the United States and France. For a schematic overview of the different disciplines that have now evolved after more than 65 years of research and development, please refer to Figure 1 at the end of this chapter.

Shortly after the Second World War, the U.S. *Department of Defense* (DoD) faced a special challenge: what kind of defence system was needed for a safer future? This implied the need to answer a secondary question as well: on what future defence system will the necessary military strategy and doctrine be based? Making a choice between the possible different types of defence systems, deciding which should be eligible for further development and public funding, was for various reasons a difficult task: the war had left an *uncertain* political situation, which still prevailed when the world entered the Cold War period in the years after 1946.

The U.S. and Great Britain, concerned with their own post-war economic problems, had remained extremely grateful to the Soviet Union for the active role they had played in ending the Second World War. However, it was the historic speech by Sir Winston Churchill (1874-1965) at Westminster College, Fulton, U.S. on 5 March 1946 that captured and emphasised the gradual change in the way the democratic West was starting to view the dictatorial communist East. The West no longer saw the Soviet Union as an ally, but as a growing military and ideological menace for freedom and democracy. Many contemporary historians consider 5 March 1946 as the beginning of the Cold War (1946-1991). Nevertheless, in 1946 many still ridiculed Sir Winston for his prophetic warning that an *iron curtain*[8] would divide the European continent.

In these circumstances, what would be the nature of future conflicts? Which military systems would be most adequate for dealing with them? In addition, the last war had also led to an unprecedented progress in science, thereby increasing the complexity of weapon systems. Consequently, the risk inherent to complex R&D-developments also increased: would this lead to the results we wanted and would these systems actually work? There was also additional uncertainty about the effectiveness of weapon systems, because this largely depended on what other nations were developing during the same period.

In short, how could the right decisions be made in this uncertain context for the selection of the defence systems to be further developed? There was clearly a need for better methods to make these decisions. Two types of need were of particular concern:

- The need for a method to achieve a reasonable consensus on future evolutions among the many and varied opinions of the military and political experts. The greater the number of experts, the greater the number of different opinions;
- The need for simulation models for various possible future environments, so that different political options and their consequences could be tested.

The first need inspired the development of the Delphi method; the second need led to the development of 'systems analysis', which in turn led to the development of 'game theory', 'war games' and, ultimately, to the scenario method. It was the *RAND Corporation* that took up this challenge and developed these new decision-making tools.

**Herman Kahn – 11 May 1965.**

*Photographer: O'Halloran, Thomas. Stored: Library of Congress, Washington D.C., US*

RAND is an acronym for Research ANd Development and it was most probably the first think-tank in the world. The institute was set up as *Project Rand*[9] by the U.S. Air Force (U.S.A.F.) in Santa Monica, California in 1946 and was subcontracted to the Douglas Aircraft Company.[10] According to one of the founders, Theodore von Kármán[11] (1881-1963), the new organization was intended to be a "think factory" that would bring and keep together a team of the "*best of the brightest*",[12] who had worked on the *Manhattan Project* (*cf.* first atomic bomb) during the Second World War. Their task was to solve the complex problems that now faced the U.S. as it entered the Cold War. In subsequent years, RAND developed new decision-making methods based on operational research, game theory and new techniques to predict the future, such as scenario planning and the Delphi method (named after the most famous oracle of the ancient world: the Oracle of the Temple of Apollo at Delphi in Greece).

The Delphi method consists of reaching consensus among a group of experts on possible evolutions or solutions for a problem that could or will occur in the future. To achieve this, each expert's arguments are considered as objectively as possible and without prejudice. Furthermore, the participating experts *do not meet and do not know who is presenting which argument*. This is designed to avoid group thinking and group domination, since it was feared – and probably correctly – that some experts with a tremendous reputation, important political influence or personal assertiveness could impose their views on the group during group discussions. In this way, they would perhaps influence the future vision too strongly.

This phenomenon of *group thinking* was actually first discovered by the Imperial German Army during the First World War and afterwards reconfirmed by the experiences of the British Army during the Second World War. They both discovered that it is actually a *very bad idea to bring experienced and highly intelligent people together in a single group at General Staff HQ to plan military operations!* Most of their plans will eventually fail – as both armies discovered to their cost in both world wars. The reason is an absence of sufficient *group diversity* among the staff members. Since too many of the group members have shared the same experiences, and therefore have the same opinions, there is not enough critical thinking and debate[13]. People with the same education, training, experience and vision find it difficult to make plans which accept that the enemy may outsmart them. Critical assumptions become implicit assumptions; the group becomes blind to alternatives. Together, they fail to think the unthinkable. Recent research on strategic thinking in turbulent environments by boards of directors has reached similar conclusions (*cf.* Chapter 4 – leadership in turbulent environments).

The process of coming to a consensus passes through several different phases. During the first phase, each expert is asked individually about his vision of the problem by means of a questionnaire. All their answers, together with their reasons for preferring certain solutions or for predicting certain evolutions, are given in writing. In a second phase, all the individual responses are shared anonymously with the whole group. The experts are then asked whether they would change their personal opinion based on the arguments made by the other (unknown) experts. The process is repeated, usually three to four times, until there is sufficient consensus between all the experts.

This Delphi method was developed to help to answer the first of the challenges mentioned above; namely, the need to achieve a reasonable consensus among experts. At the same time, another method was designed to answer the second challenge; the need to make simulation models, which is known as *systems analysis* (*cf.* Ludwig von Bertalanffy).

Systems analysis is used to assist decision-makers in solving complex problems with highly uncertain outcomes; hence the use of simulation models. The current scenario planning techniques are based on this method. The brilliant mind behind these developments at RAND was Herman Kahn (1922-1983).[14]

Initially, when working at RAND, Kahn elaborated future scenarios for the U.S.A.F. Air Defense System Missile Command. He was responsible for the development of the so-called *early warning systems* (EWS) for controlling anti-aircraft missiles. The term EWS is still used today for capturing signals that lead to the elaboration and evaluation of a particular future scenario. Kahn's genius and talent only became fully apparent in the 1960s, when he criticized U.S. nuclear strategy for a lack of realism. He contradicted the leading U.S. military strategists, arguing that their planning tended to be based on wishful thinking rather than on reasonable expectations. He based his criticism on scenarios that explored (*cf.* explorative scenarios) the future horizon in broad terms and demonstrated that the U.S. nuclear strategy would probably lead to a nuclear war, as a result of making wrong assessments of the available data. As an alternative, Kahn advocated a thorough sense of reality based on facts and logic, which he summarized in the famous phrase: *"thinking about the unthinkable"*. Because of this, he was a major influence on the Pentagon in the 1950s and 1960s. In 1960, he published his notable and much debated book: *On Thermonuclear War,* a title that deliberately parodied the famous book of Carl von Clausewitz (1780-1831) *On War (Vom Kriege),* published in 1832. A year later in 1961, Kahn left the RAND Corporation to establish the Hudson Institute, where he applied scenario-based thinking to social forecasting problems and public policy support. This led to his most controversial book, published together with Anthony Wiener in 1967: *The year 2000. A framework for speculation on the next thirty-three years.* This book introduced to strategic management literature one of the earliest definitions of 'scenarios' as a methodological tool for policy planning and decision-making processes in complex and uncertain environments. Even today, it is still considered a milestone in the field of scenario planning. Because of this 1967 book, Herman Kahn is often referred to as the father of modern-day scenario-based thinking in literature.

A few years after Kahn's departure, the researchers Olaf Helmer (1910-2011) and Theodore (Ted) Gordon – who were both inspired by Kahn's and Wiener's work – also left RAND. Together with former RAND and internet pioneer Paul Baran (1926-2011), they founded the *Institute for the Future* (IFTF) in California in 1968. Helmer and Gordon experimented together with researchers from the *Futures Group* of the *Stanford Research Institute* and the *Californian Institute of Technology* to use scenarios as a planning tool. As a result, they became widely known as pioneers in the field of future research in the U.S. The work of Helmer and Gordon at the IFTF led to the development of new methods such as *trends-impact analysis* (TIA) and *cross-impact analysis* (CIA).[15]

Even though these TIA and CIA methods were mostly developed in conjunction with the Delphi method, current practice is mostly based on the *cross impact systems* and the *matrices method* developed in 1974 in France by Jean-Claude Duperrin and Michel Godet. This method starts with a series of $n$ subsequently occurring future events. Each event $n$ receives an *a priori* probability (*cf.* Bayes' theorem), estimated by a group of experts. If we consider $n$ subsequent events, then the possible number of interactions between these events $n$ is $2^n$. The number of possible interactions not only generates a huge number of possible scenarios with increasing $n$, but also causes an increasing number of possible inconsistencies. Consistency can still be achieved by demanding that all the estimated *a priori* probabilities fulfil the basic axioms of probability theory. In this way, it becomes possible to calculate in a consistent manner the most likely and most probable sequence of events and, by so doing, makes it possible to rank the different scenarios based on their likelihood or probability of occurrence. This method is still a basic technique for estimating technological trends.

The work of Helmer, Gordon and Herman Kahn was picked up by industry; in particular, by Pierre Wack at Royal Dutch Shell.

In 1967, Shell initiated a *Year 2000 Study* in which they tried to predict the context of the oil industry in the year 2000. The study proved to be very relevant. It brought to light that discontinuities could and might emerge in the oil industry and suggested that the unbroken period of expansion that the sector had experienced annually would not continue until 1985, let alone until the year 2000.

Pierre Wack (1922-1997), who was a business planner at Shell in France, was instructed to look at these findings in more depth, this time limiting his study to the year 1985. The new project was named *Horizon Planning*. Although the method used for elaborating on the different scenarios was still primitive, the study brought clear confirmation of the *Year 2000* exercise. As a result, Shell decided to further experiment with scenario-based thinking. They realized that the conventional predictions, used elsewhere in the industry as a planning instrument, would most probably be wrong if the predicted discontinuity came to pass.

The new method turned out to be an exceptionally successful innovation: in 1972, the study was presented to the senior management of the group with the conclusion that a shortage of oil would arise and that this would lead to strong price increases. Today we know what happened during the next few years, which saw the start of a series of oil crises. But at the time, none of the traditional prediction techniques could have given management this insight.

The work of Kahn, Helmer and Gordon, but also of Norman Dalkey, Pierre Wack and Peter Schwartz of the *Stanford Research Institute*, laid the foundations of what is today referred to as the 'Intuitive Logics School' of scenario planning (*cf.* chapter 3), which is now an integral part of strategy management and business planning literature.

Also in the 1950s, while Herman Kahn was making scenarios for the U.S. Army, the French philosopher Gaston Berger (1896-1960) founded in Paris *Le Centre d'Etudes Prospectives*. From 1957 onwards, this Centre for Prospective Studies used scenario-based thinking to develop long-term planning. Berger gave his centre the pet name *La Prospective*. He also introduced the use of the word 'prospective' as a noun, which he defined as "the study of possible futures" (*études des futurs possibles*). In a 1957 publication he explained, described and justified the use of the new noun as follows:

> "Our civilization only detaches itself with difficulty from its fascination with the past. It only has dreams of the future, and when developing projects that are no longer mere dreams, it draws them on a canvas where the past is still projected. Our civilization is stubbornly retrospective, whereas it should be 'prospective'."[m6]

Berger founded his centre out of a sense of dissatisfaction; in particular, dissatisfaction about the short-sightedness of the traditional prediction methods, which start from the implicit assumption that the future is just an extrapolation of the past and that therefore discontinuities cannot occur. But his motivation as a philosopher went even deeper: he could not accept that the long-term social and political future of France was foreordained by the country's past. Berger, who worked previously as an industrial adviser and civil servant at the French Ministry of Education, believed in a possible future that can be consciously modelled for the benefit of mankind. Little wonder, then, that Berger focused on normative scenarios for a positive future, which he subsequently launched into the political arena. His idea was to offer policy-makers a vision for a (better) future. It was then up to the politicians to put this into action.

Gaston Berger (who, incidentally, was the father of the well-known choreographer Maurice Béjart)[17] died in 1960. But his centre continued to carry out its pioneering work. In the 1960s and 1970s, he was succeeded by two very special individuals: Baron Bertrand de Jouvenel des Ursins and Pierre Massé.

Bertrand de Jouvenel (1903-1987) – the renowned author of *On Power: the natural history of its growth* (*cf. Du Pouvoir*), a standard work on the mechanisms of power in politics and worldwide mandatory reading for political sciences students – was a French philosopher, professor, political scientist, lawyer, economist and futurist. By 1960, he had already founded the Paris-based *Futuribles International*,[18] led today by his son Hugues. He joined the *Centre d'Etudes Prospectives* in 1966.

Pierre Massé (1898-1987), a brilliant student of the famous elite French civil service schools *Ecole Polytechnique* and *Ecole Nationale des Ponts et Chaussées,* was trained as both a civil engineer and an economist. This multitalented man was simultaneously a civil servant, a captain of industry and an academic professor. He was later elected to the French National Academy – becoming an *Académicien*[19] *et Membre de l'Institut de France* – in 1977. He was the third commissioner in charge of *Le Commissariat Général du Plan* (CGP or Central Planning Commission) from 1959 till 1966. This French institute for economic analysis and planning was established in 1946 by General Charles de Gaulle, based on a proposal from Jean Monnet, who became its first commissioner from 1946 till 1952. It is this very same Jean Omer Marie Gabriel Monnet (1888-1979) who is now considered as one of the architects of European unity and a founding father of the European Union (E.U.) (*cf.* Monnet Plan, European Coal and Steel Community). The CGP would play a significant role in the reconstruction of the French economy in the post-war period. Pierre Massé introduced prospective scenario techniques to format French national economic plans from the year 1960 onwards.[20]

Bertrand de Jouvenel thought that too many small and dominant political groups with a very narrow vision of the future were determining the destiny of France. He argued that this could be avoided, if forward-looking thinkers like him were allowed to sketch idealistic images of what that future might bring – images that could serve as a blueprint for the nation. Bertrand de Jouvenel used scenario-based thinking to develop *scientific utopias* that sketched a positive vision of the future. He also specified how these utopias could be put into practice, so that the lives of ordinary people could be improved.

Jouvenel formulated the hypothesis that while it is perhaps impossible to predict the future based on scientifically discovered laws that might one day lead to a 'science of the future', it is nevertheless perfectly possible to think about the future in a scientific way by taking into account all possible scientific knowledge acquired from such disciplines as mathematics, complexity and chaos theory, psychology, economics, decision-making, neuroscience, *etc.*

## Contemporary futures research

*Futures research* is the scientific discipline that conducts research into the laws governing the future and its predictability. This body of knowledge has grown from two different schools of thought: firstly, the U.S. school based around the RAND

Corporation, with pioneers such as Kahn, Helmer and Gordon; secondly, the French prospective school based around Berger, Massé, de Jouvenel and Godet. Futures research as a separate discipline has evolved over the last seventy years to become a multidisciplinary science involving economics, public policy, sociology, history, political science, psychology, mathematics, biology, geology, technology, engineering and even architecture. Philosophy and theology have recently been integrated as well. The central focus of present-day futures research is *complexity theory*.

Using this multidisciplinary approach, futures research examines in a systematic way past and present data (often non-deterministic), patterns, relationships and causes, as well as the underlying worldview of assumptions. The aim is to examine how past or current relationships may influence, determine or change the likelihood of possible future events and trends. In addition, attention is devoted to understanding long-term challenges and attempts are made to anticipate future fundamental changes, based on an insight of what is likely to stay the same and what might reasonably be expected to change. This methodology includes 'thinking about', 'debates on' and 'forms of' possible futures. Through this approach scientists are able to contribute in a critical way to the taking of complex decisions.

Futures research is not about short-term forecasts or predictions of trends such as interest rates, oil prices, stock prices, *etc.*; nor is it about operational plans or short-term business plans. Futures research is a science looking at postulates about 'potential', 'plausible', 'desirable' or 'preferable' futures. This approach is summarized in the so-called *3 Ps – possible, plausible and preferable*. The existence of these 3 Ps is closely related to and usually the result of 'strategic shocks' (*cf.* future shocks, wildcards or black swans): events with a low probability of occurrence but with very high impact or serious consequences. Futures research or the study of the future is often classified academically as a discipline of the social sciences and is seen as being complementary to history, which is the study of the past. Scientifically based futures research is also known as *futures studies* or *strategic foresight*. Other terms used in the literature include *futures thinking* and *futurology* (not to be confused with science fiction).

The oldest futures research journal is probably *World Futures*, published by Taylor & Francis since 1962. Over the past 50 years, several other leading scientific journals have been established. The most influential of today's academic journals are: *Futures*; *Technological Forecasting and Social Change (TFSC)*; and *Long Range Planning (LRP)*. These three scientific journals are *Web of Science* (WoS) indexed and have been published by Elsevier since 1969. Sage Publications started issuing of the scientific journal *World Future Review* in 2009 and Springer launched the online open access *European Journal of Futures Research (EJFR)* (http://ejfr.eu) in 2013.

Leading international research centres currently include:

- *World Future Society* (www.wfs.org), the largest membership society for futures, publishing the magazine *The Futurist* since 1967 and, in collaboration with Sage, the *World Future Review* since 2009.
- *Futuribles* (Paris)(www.futuribles.com), publishing *Futuribles* since 1975.
- *World Futures Studies Federation* (www.wfsf.org).
- *Institute for the Future* (Palo Alto, California) (www.iftf.org).
- *National Intelligence Council*, affiliated to the *Office of the Director of National Intelligence,* Washington DC, U.S. (www.dni.gov/nic/NIC_home.html).
- *The Millennium Project – Global Futures Intelligence System* (http://millennium-project.org).

Futures research is a science mainly used by governments, corporations and companies to support critical and complex decision-making in the areas of strategic policy formulation or strategic risk management (*cf.* Figure 15).

# Summary

1.  The environment in which policy and companies operate has thoroughly changed in recent times. It is characterized by:

    -   Increasing complexity
    -   Increasing speed of change
    -   Increasing uncertainty

2.  The instruments that were used in the past for policy and business are inadequate for this new environment because:

    -   They start from the premise that the future is a continuation of the past and that discontinuities are impossible;
    -   They hide premises and risks instead of explicitly exposing them;
    -   The available information is in itself insufficient. The key lies in the interpretation of the (future) environment: we must learn to observe, to monitor and to re-interpret.

3.  The method of future thinking is a better tool to prepare for the future. It is an academic and an arts-based method that enables better anticipation of future uncertainties, complex problems and rapid changes.

4.  Modern techniques of future thinking had their origin in the period following the Second World War. They were developed almost simultaneously in the United States and France. The applications have evolved from military problems of national security to business challenges and public policy issues.

## Figure 1: Overview of the development of scenario methodologies

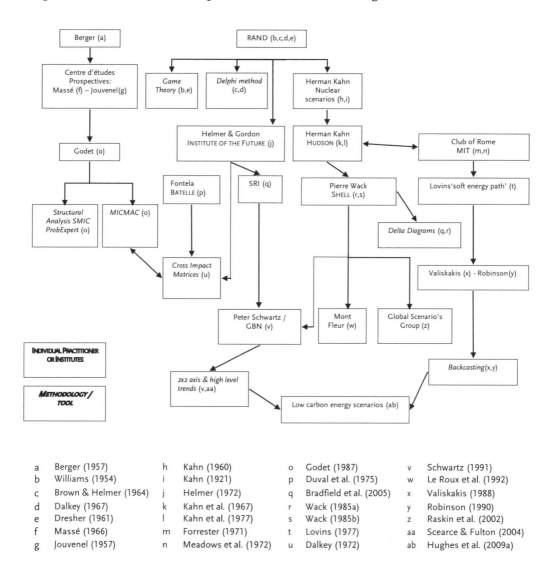

| | | | | |
|---|---|---|---|---|
| a | Berger (1957) | h | Kahn (1960) | o | Godet (1987) | v | Schwartz (1991) |

a   Berger (1957)          h   Kahn (1960)              o   Godet (1987)             v    Schwartz (1991)
b   Williams (1954)        i   Kahn (1921)              p   Duval et al. (1975)      w    Le Roux et al. (1992)
c   Brown & Helmer (1964)  j   Helmer (1972)            q   Bradfield et al. (2005)  x    Valiskakis (1988)
d   Dalkey (1967)          k   Kahn et al. (1967)       r   Wack (1985a)             y    Robinson (1990)
e   Dresher (1961)         l   Kahn et al. (1977)       s   Wack (1985b)             z    Raskin et al. (2002)
f   Massé (1966)           m   Forrester (1971)         t   Lovins (1977)            aa   Scearce & Fulton (2004)
g   Jouvenel (1957)        n   Meadows et al. (1972)    u   Dalkey (1972)            ab   Hughes et al. (2009a)

*Source:* based on Hughes, N. (2009).

# Chapter 2
# **About wicked problems**

*"The practitioner must choose: shall he remain on the high ground solving unimportant problems according to prevailing standards of rigour, or shall he descend to the swamp of important problems and non-rigorous inquiry?"*
Donald A. Schön (1930-1997)

## The use of future thinking

When does the future really become relevant? That is the question we will attempt to answer in this chapter.

*The chairwoman of the board of directors thought that exceptional circumstances would require exceptional measures. She was head of a leading company that had discovered a whole range of new medicines through world-class research and had been able to bring them to market successfully.*

*However, dark storm clouds were now gathering on the horizon and an extraordinary meeting of the board of directors would have to discuss urgently the situation. Because this was different. Different from all the other challenges she had faced and conquered in her impressive career. This time she could neither properly grasp nor define the problem. During the past few months there had indeed been a number of difficulties that she thought were coincidental: actual costs exceeded predicted costs for the development of a new breakthrough in active molecules, since the project took longer than expected. Likewise, actual sales were lower than projected sales. Perhaps this was due to the economic crisis? This was why she had already issued instructions to reduce operational costs, investments and cash expenditure. It was not pleasant, but she had courageously made the necessary cuts.*

*Unfortunately the situation continued to deteriorate quarter after quarter. Each time, new and additional cost reduction was required. She had now decided that an even more drastic cut in the costs still needed to be made. She hoped that this ultimate intervention would turn the tide quickly.*

*The latest quarterly results had hit like a bombshell: still no research breakthrough, still disappointing sales figures. This time more thorough questions about the results were raised: where does this end? Is this a cyclical phenomenon? Is this a temporary crisis? Would further slimming down be enough this time?*

*A combination of adverse elements threatened the company's success formula. Investments in research, driven by the rapid increase in complexity, needed to be increased continuously. Discovering active molecules now seemed to take longer and longer and the risks were getting bigger and bigger. As a result, every month large amounts of money were probably wasted on this research, with growing uncertainty about the final outcomes. On top of all this, the patents on a number of existing drugs would end in the near future and everyone knew what this meant: cheaper generic drugs would immediately hit the market, taking a huge bite out of the income stream.*

*Just like Sir David, who could not fully understand the unprecedented spread of foot-and-mouth disease, this director also had a 'wicked' problem for which she could not immediately formulate either an action plan or an approach. It all went too fast, the complexity was too great and uncertainty seemed to increase all the time. What gradually became apparent was that the combination of these elements could tarnish the success formula of the company. So what did she need to do?*

## Wicked problems: a problem with problems

Keith Grint, a professor of leadership at Warwick Business School and an associate fellow at Green Templeton College in Oxford refers to this class of problems as *wicked problems*.[21]

Wicked problems are by nature confusing and difficult to define or explain. Grint also says that wicked problems are problems with *clumsy solutions*. It pays to look at his research findings.

Grint was investigating how problems that were affecting organizations could be organized according to the environment or context in which the problems occurred. In other words, he was studying how the relationship between *context – problem – leadership* would change depending on the type of context or problem.

This was a judicious approach. In the 1990s, Roquebert and his colleagues from Texas Tech University already conducted research into the relationship with the context. They wanted to understand to what extent management actions determine the fate of a company and to what extent the performance of a company is determined by the context. Roquebert's approach was to calculate the performance[22] of company resources over time. He did this for more than 100 companies in 160 different industry sectors. What did he find? Well, 45% of the explainable variation in performance was related to external contextual effects, largely driven by industrial sector changes and, to a lesser extent, by political and social changes. Only 55% of the variation was attributable to specific company management actions. If we were to repeat this study today, after more than a decade of globalization and after the financial crisis of 2008, one would expect management actions to have even a smaller impact on company performance and hence on the future of the company. Actually, a study of this kind was carried out by Derrick Gosselin in 2014 at Ghent University. Gosselin applied the same method as Roquebert to more than 120 Belgian companies. What did he find? Surprisingly, and notwithstanding 20 years of globalization and increased turbulence, the *ratio* between external factors (45%) and internal factors (55%) had remained roughly constant! However, the origins of the 45% of external factors had become to a large extent unpredictable, whereas in the Roquebert study a high proportion was related to the industry sector. This means that the context has become much more *uncertain* (*cf.* causal texture), while the impact of management actions on performance remains at the same level of 55%.

We believe that two lessons can be drawn from both studies: firstly, the leaders of companies and perhaps also of organizations, should spend much more time on context, because this determines more than half of performance and the results of the company, and therefore the dividends and value creation expected by shareholders! Secondly, since context has become much more uncertain, new methods for dealing with strategic uncertainty and risk should be introduced as part of corporate governance.

The contextual characterization of Grint is therefore relevant: he concluded that problems dependent on the environment can be defined into three main types: critical problems, tamed problems and wicked problems. We will now look briefly at each of these three types.

## 1. The critical problem

A critical problem is clearly recognizable and typically occurs on a tactical level, often related to urgencies or crisis situations. There is a degree of uncertainty, but seemingly not in the eyes of the leader who formulates the problem and takes the decisions. Experience with this type of problem has shown that there is no time for discussions or disagreements. Coercion is used and, given the circumstances, is also legitimate. Critical problems are best handled through hierarchical structures, based on unity of command and control, while motivation is best encouraged by rewards. Examples of a critical problem are a train collision, a military attack, a car accident or fighting a fire. The problem is clearly recognizable, the emergency services arrive on the scene and the commanding officer tells everyone what must happen. Between two crises, the organization will primarily concentrate on the problems they expect to deal with in the future and will train to gain further experience and faster speed of intervention and execution. The role of the commanding officer is to dictate what should be done. When a critical problem arises, he or she gives an answer to that problem.

## 2. The tamed problem

A tamed problem is more complex in nature. Think of a puzzle. Although a puzzle can seem very complicated, there is always only one correct solution. Examples include the formatting of schedules, heart surgery, the construction of a factory or the launch of a new product. These activities may all be very complex, but they are not a *first of a kind* (FOAK) or a *very first of a kind* (VFOAK) type of problem. Often these problems have been handled before and hence a process is available to address them. In other words, there is a known, rational and logical process that can be managed. The role of management is therefore to organize and document an adequate process and methodology to solve the problem.

## 3. The wicked problem

A wicked problem[23] occurs in a context where there is a high degree of uncertainty, continuous and rapid change, and high levels of complexity. Examples include the post-war reconstruction of Iraq, dealing with Afghanistan after 11 September 2001 (*cf.* New York, 9/11 terrorist attacks), preparations for terrorist attacks or dealing with climate change. Strategy formulation and business modelling for entrepreneurial high-tech ventures, commercial expansion in risky countries, investment in emerging technologies and fundamental basic research also fall into this category. The uncertainty and ambiguity cannot be reduced through further and 'better' analysis. The complexity increases because the problem cannot be solved by isolation or reduction. It involves several domains and hierarchical structures, and it runs through different systems. There is no known, rational and logical process to solve these problems, as there is for tamed problems. It is a new problem or a problem that continues to persist; for example, when the initial problem generates new problems time after time.

For wicked problems, there is no single solution. It is often difficult to define the problem or, worse still, to determine the boundaries and the extent of the problem. This is consistent with the wisdom imparted by some professors to their Ph.D. students that they will only be able to fully understand, grasp and define their research questions once they have finished their doctoral thesis!

Consider the Iraq problem. What is the most important issue? Perhaps security? If so, an effective police force should be urgently created. Or does this security depend more on neighbouring countries that finance terrorist groups? If so, the priority should be to develop good relations with these countries. Or should there first be mediation, in order to create trust between the rival Shiite, Sunni and Kurdish groups? You could also argue that poverty is a breeding ground for terrorism, so that it seems sensible to repair the nation's damaged infrastructure as quickly as possible, thereby generating both oil revenue and local employment.

There are no right, good, wrong or bad solutions: only better or worse developments. Sometimes finding a solution is subordinate to finding a consensus on the approach. These types of problems are more driven by the process than by the solution.

The role of leaders in these circumstances is to ask the right questions and to organize committed cooperation and discussion. These are not management problems. They are leadership problems, where collaboration is necessary. Leadership in relation to a wicked problem requires a different interpretation than what we would usually mean by 'strong leadership' in turbulent times.[24] In fact, it requires precisely the opposite. We do not need a hero commander, who proclaims a single 'right way' that reflects the official policy line. The focus here must be on asking the right questions and on the continuous monitoring and reinterpretation of the future environment. In Chapter 4 we will explore this new form of leadership for dealing with wicked problems.

*So what happened at the extraordinary meeting of the board of directors of our pharmaceutical company? Well, it was difficult. Many questions were asked. Why hadn't they noticed the discontinuity in research output and the decrease in turnover earlier? What if this was not a critical problem, for which temporary crisis measures would suffice? Where would the resizing end? Nobody could answer these questions. "What are we going to do if this situation continues?" asked one director in desperation. A simple exclamation, but one which asked the fundamental question about the validity of the assumptions behind the company's business model for the future.*

*The meeting ended in complete confusion. Nobody understood what was happening; no one could identify the problem or knew when it would end; nobody could say how the situation would evolve or how the company should react. But the seriousness of the situation was clear to all: the future of the business was at stake. The directors eventually decided to assign a working group the task of drawing up proposals for the next meeting. Secretly, many of them hoped that by then the figures would have returned to normal and that the current unrest had just been an unnecessary panic...*

## When is the use of future thinking appropriate?

- When testing strategic options.
- When testing the *robustness* of a strategy and testing business models in the different scenarios.

- When new and unprecedented hypotheses need to be developed and tested on their validity.
- When the problem is intractable and difficult to define or when insight in understanding the problem is essential.
- When the complexity of the situation is too great to take immediate action. First, the complexity must be reduced, a process in which gaining a better understanding of the context plays a key role.
- When redefining difficult problems.
- When changing the culture of the organization.
- When anticipating new events (in circumstances where past predictions are no longer usable, because there are too many differences with the past).
- When searching for and developing innovations and new options.
- When the discussions with *stakeholders* need to be improved, to allow the company to respond to a situation more effectively.
- When the learning behaviour of the organization must improve.
- When attempting to identify uncertainties and risks.
- When the future orientation of a group, occupation, region or country is at stake.
- When developing a common language to express thinking and to increase the quality of discussion.
- When different and contradictory opinions exist about the course that should be taken but constructive solutions need to be formed.
- When more confidence is needed before action can be taken.
- When forming a vision, including the influence of the environment.
- For teambuilding.
- For the creation of a better future or world.

Before we proceed to the next section of the book, in which we will discuss this approach in more detail, we will first make three digressions to look at the insights of three exceptional scientists – Richard Nisbett, Philip Tetlock and Herman Kahn – who spent most of their professional lives investigating the way people look at their surroundings.

People actually differ in how they observe, interpret and react to their environment. Consequently, it is fascinating to examine the factors that determine how people read their environment and also to understand why some people put these observations into action, while others with the same observations do nothing.

## People see other environments or see the same environments differently

*Why do people read their environment in different ways?*

As a professor of social psychology at the University of Michigan at Ann Arbor, Richard E. Nisbett noticed that his Asian students sometimes had a very different manner of looking at reality than his American or Western students. Nisbett is an experimental psychologist and was fascinated by these differences. He asked himself: *"Does our cultural background affect our behaviour and the way we look at and interpret our surroundings?"* A good question – but how do you uncover these differences?

He devised an experiment that would not only shed light on this subject, but also start a completely new branch of scientific research literature as well. Nisbett projected a series of images with the same basic pattern: each image showed a large object against a realistic but complex background; for example, a tiger in a dense forest or a horse in a field of flowers.

Students who took part in the study were asked to view the images and their eye movement was monitored by a special device. Nisbett was able to observe exactly how his students looked at the images. He first performed the experiment with a group of students who were raised in the U.S. and he then did the same with students who had spent their youth in China and Japan.

The results were astonishing: there was a significant difference between the way U.S. and Eastern students looked at the images. The western-educated U.S. students immediately focused on the object (the horse, the tiger), while the Chinese and Japanese students concentrated on the context (the field, the forest).

Nisbett then went a step further. After the slide show, he asked the students what they remembered about the images. The western-educated students immediately listed the objects they had seen: a horse, a tiger, a dolphin, *etc.* But the eastern-educated students did precisely the opposite: they recalled the backgrounds, with a forest or a floral meadow. Often, they even forgot which object was in the foreground!

Nisbett next decided to do a follow-up experiment. This time, he projected the same images, but he switched the background and the objects. For example, the students were shown a tiger in a field of flowers or a horse in a forest. This produced an even more remarkable finding: many of the eastern students said that they had not seen these objects in the earlier test! Apparently, they could only recall the backgrounds. Nisbett completed his experiment with the U.S. students. He projected the same objects as before, but this time with a slightly modified background. For example, the flower field now had other colours (say, from the colours of spring to the colours of autumn). The majority of the American students did not see any change in the images.

So what are the reasons for these differences and what possible lessons can we learn from this?

According to Nisbett, the main reasons why Western and Eastern people look and behave differently towards their environment and context are rooted in differences in culture, social structure and education. People raised and educated in a Western culture tend to have considerably more options, choice and autonomy in their lives. They can often pursue their own interests, while paying little attention to other people's concerns. They are analytical thinkers. Their education makes them focus on logic, rationality and scientifically-based thinking, an environment in which the exchange and discussion of ideas are highly valued and stimulated. Furthermore, they see, think and focus on a single object, noticing its specific attributes, following which they group, analyse, and categorise the object on the basis of those attributes (cf. taxonomy).[25] They think inductively through generalisations and search for universal laws in order to model and control their reality. Westerners have a very high sense of control, even if it is sometimes illusory. Moreover, Westerners presume that their universal laws are *deterministic* (*i.e.* always applicable) and *linear* (*i.e.* running in a continuous line, so that the future can always be extrapolated from the past). They use this logic to evaluate propositions (including propositions that require thinking about future evolutions, as in cases of strategic decision-making). This free, scientific and analytical way of thinking goes back to the ancient Greeks, with their remarkable sense of logic, classification, taxonomic schemes and personal agency. Westerners are more individualistic and independent, and so they focus more on the object they want to control.

In contrast, the equally ancient and advanced civilization of China placed much more emphasis on harmony with others than on freedom of individual action. This culture is therefore based on a much broader focus on the field or context in which objects are located. It is the relationship between the object and the field that is used to predict and explain behaviour. Easterners have little concern with universal laws; consequently, the notion of control is something difficult for them to grasp. They do not think in linear terms but in circular terms (a trend will eventually bend) and they have no cultural tradition with formal logic, preferring instead they focus on a *dialectic* approach: if confronted with two opposed propositions, they will try to find a way to accommodate them both. Easterners are more collectivist or interdependent; hence their need to focus on others. Easterners also have a more holistic view: they *see other things* because they *focus on other things*, including the relationship between objects.

Richard Nisbett believes that this more focused and more egocentric way of European thinking leads to what he calls the "fundamental attribution error" (FAE). This is a failure to recognize that situational forces may explain both our present behaviour and future evolutions, so that possible different futures – and not just a single, deterministic, logic-based and extrapolated future – must first be considered. Western-educated leaders frequently make this fundamental attribution error when they assume that future behaviour will reflect the dispositions they deduce from present behaviour.[26] The difference in attention to context between Westerners and Easterners also means that Easterners have a preference for situational explanations, whereas Westerners are more likely to explain things in dispositional terms (*i.e.* personal and individual-related factors).

The implications of this research for everyday life are profound. People with a European cultural background and education need to pay more attention to context. This will improve the likelihood that they will correctly identify situational factors that influence future evolutions and behaviour. Furthermore, they should realize that situational factors frequently influence our behaviour and that of others more deeply than they seem to do, whereas dispositional factors are usually less influential than they seem. In our ever more rapidly changing world, the question of whether Western (*i.e.* European) culture – with its lack of attention to changes in context – is more or less beneficial than Oriental culture, seems more than justified. This is especially true for assessing complex wicked problems. The direct, egocentric, deterministic and linear way of Western thinking can sometimes be perilous. You want proof? Just remember the *'Bomb Iraq'* or *'Do something'* slogans on the banners aimed at President George W. Bush after 09/11!

## About 'foxes' and 'hedgehogs'

There is another thought-provoking insight from a very different domain that can help us to understand how we interpret the environment around us. The invasion of Iraq in 2003 was the result of a number of erroneous decisions, based on wrong assessments, analysis and estimates made by intelligence services, experts, academics and politicians alike. How was it possible that the opinions of all these experts were so completely wrong? In fact, this should have come as no surprise. If one assesses the overall effectiveness of the Central Intelligence Agency (CIA), created in 1947 to prevent strategic surprises during the rapidly escalating Cold War, a similar pattern of misinterpretation is visible across several decades. The CIA failed to predict and warn the U.S. Government about all four of the most important crises since the end of the Second World War: the Cuban Missile crisis (1962), the Tet Offensive during the Vietnam War (1968), the fall of the Berlin Wall (1989) and the attack on the *World Trade Center* (11 September 2001, WTC Towers, New York) (*cf.* Jones & Silberzahn, 2013). And on each occasion, this failure was rooted in a lack of understanding of the wider context.

Not that the Americans or the CIA are unique in this respect. In 1953, the French *général de corps d'armée* Henri Eugène Navarre (1898-1983), commander-in-chief of the French forces in Indochina, decided to establish a garrison in the Tonkin region at *Dien Bien Phu*, located in the heart of Viet Minh-held territory in the Muong Thanh Valley, just a short distance from the border with Laos (*cf.* operation Castor). This decision shows the same pattern of refusal to consider all possible options. Deliberately selected for its location, General Navarre was convinced that the plain of Dien Bien Phu, surrounded as it was by steep jungle-covered mountains and hills, could never be taken. In fact, he was certain that it would prove to be an excellent site to apply the so-called 'hedgehog' tactic: faced with the loss of this strategically important position, the Viet Minh would be forced to attack and would be destroyed by superior French firepower. This tactic was first designed by the German Army during the Second World War and had been proven to be very effective in the plains of Russia. The French were actually concerned that the Viet

Minh would not dare to attack! But they need not have worried... Dien Bien Phu turned out to be the single most decisive battle in the conflict, ending the French presence in South-East Asia through the Geneva Accord of 1954, which partitioned Indochina into North and South Vietnam. This would eventually lead to the collapse of the French Colonial Empire within the next 10 years and was destined to have a major impact on geopolitics during the following decades. The military and political disaster of Dien Bien Phu was so great that its impact is regarded as comparable in French history to the defeats at Sedan (1870), Waterloo (1815) or Agincourt (1415).

The artillery commander at Dien Bien Phu, Lieutenant Colonel Charles Piroth (1906-1954), when confronted with the possibility that the Viet Minh could bring in artillery to the surrounding hills and thereby create a death-trap for the French Army by cutting off its aerial supply line, replied with a confidence that soon turned out to be misplaced. Firstly, he claimed, it would be impossible for the Viet Minh to install heavy artillery on the steep and jungle-covered hills that surrounded the base, although he did concede that a small number of light artillery pieces might be possible. Secondly, even if they did manage to bring up light pieces, these would soon be destroyed by the heavier French guns. Thirdly, even if this for some unforeseen reason proved not to be possible, the Viet Minh could never bring up enough ammunition to threaten the security of the airstrip. Or so he thought. When the battle started on 13 March 1954, the Viet Minh opened up with three days of heavy bombardments. Contrary to expectations, they had indeed managed to bring in heavy artillery, including anti-aircraft guns, through the difficult terrain along the rear slopes of the mountains surrounding the French positions. What's more, they had dug tunnels into the mountains, into which they now placed these guns, overlooking the French encampment. This made their artillery nearly impervious to French counter-battery fire – as Charles Piroth soon found out to his cost. Shamed and depressed by his failure, he committed suicide on 15 March 1954, just two days into the battle. It still took until 7 May for the base to fall, but fall it did.

It was only after the disaster that the French military came to see the weakness of their strategy at Dien Bien Phu. They started to comprehend that they had systematically rejected as a thinkable option the possibility that the surrounding mountains could be used for artillery action. Even so, if the French had evacuated Dien Bien Phu during the first days of the battle, they could have won an important tactical victory. The entire Viet Minh Army was immobilized at Dien Bien

Phu, lacking the capability to redeploy quickly. In contrast, the French had the advantage of mobility and could therefore move quickly to attack other undefended key positions of the Viet Minh. But this crucial 'second chance' was also missed.

Numerous examples of similar blinkered thinking litter our history – some of them brilliantly described by Barbara Wertheim Tuchman (1912-1989) in her book *The March of Folly* or more recently by Marc Ferro in *L'Aveuglement*.

So what exactly determines our way of correctly reading our environment? It took Philip Eyrikson Tetlock[27] many years of research to come up with the answer. He asked himself this basic question: "*Why are experts so often wrong in their predictions and how can we make better predictions?*"

His question not only applies to the assessment of political situations, like the situation in Iraq, but also to the predictions of economic experts and stock-market analysts, who have also been consistently wide of the mark in recent years. Consider, for example, the prediction of the International Monetary Fund (IMF) in October 2008, when they expected a growth rate of 3.0% for 2009. Three months later there was suddenly negative growth of -0.5%; another three months later and this had already fallen to -1.3%!

Tetlock set up a vast research project, which lasted for more than 20 years. During this time, he studied 82,361 predictions made by pundits, in order to discover the relationship between how experts think and the correctness or accuracy of their predictions. In other words, he wanted to know who was right, who was wrong and why. When he had finished, Tetlock tried to make his own predictions about the quality of the experts' predictions. He finally wrote his findings in an excellent book published in 2006: *Expert Political Judgment: how good is it? How can we know?*

To conduct his experiment on a scientific basis, Tetlock began by interviewing hundreds of experts. He asked them to make a series of predictions for the next five years: predictions about politics, about the economy and about social problems. At the end of the five years, he evaluated which predictions were right and which were wrong. In the meantime, he busied himself by organizing his interviewees into all the different possible categories he could think of: level of education, social origin, gender, optimists and pessimists, politically left or right wing, *etc.*

There are a number of tough problems to overcome when designing a scientific experiment aimed at testing judgements on future events. Actually there are two: first and foremost, forecasts are done widely without mentioning an explicit time-line. The advantage being of course that it makes them untestable over time! Or like an old and wise professor once advised: "*When challenged to make statements about the future such as economic outlooks or political predictions, be sure never to mention what will happen and when it will happen at the same time!*" By separating the *what* from the *when* a prediction becomes simply untestable. The second problem is to measure the likelihood that an event will happen. Just for the sake of the argument: when someone tells you that there exists a "serious possibility" or "a fair chance" that something could happen: what specific probabilities does one have in mind?

**Table 1: Probabilities associated with forecast expressions**

| Probabilities | Variance | The General Area of Possibility |
|---|---|---|
| 100% | | Certain |
| 93% | 6% | Almost certain |
| 75% | 12% | Probable |
| 50% | 10% | Chances about even |
| 30% | 10% | Probably not |
| 7% | 5% | Almost certainly not |
| 0% | | Impossible |

*Source:* based on Tetlock, P & Gardner, D. (2015).

Solutions to these two problems were proposed by Sherman Kent[28] (1903-1986) and by Glenn W. Brier (1913-1998). Sherman Kent defined in a chart (*cf.* Table 1) the relationship between verbal forecast expressions and their corresponding numerical probability (including their associated variance or confidence interval). In 1950 Brier proposed the mathematics to measure the distance between what is forecasted and what actually happened. He defined the so-called *Brier Score*[29] which is perhaps the most commonly used verification measure for assessing the accuracy of probability based forecasts (*cf.* Figure 2).

**Figure 2: Forecast accuracy measurement**

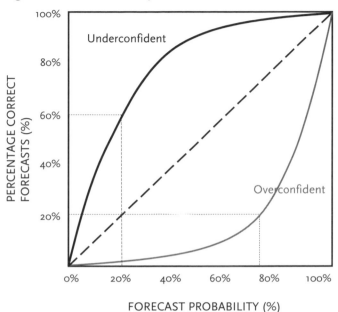

*Source:* based on Tetlock, P & Gardner, D. (2015).

Actually most leaders, opinion makers, politicians, managers resisted the wisdom of Kent to express estimates in percentages: too many political barriers, especially when reputations are at stake! However, study after study shows that people attach very different meanings to probabilistic language like "could", "might" and "likely". These words say something is possible, but they say nothing about the probability of that possibility. Almost anything "may" happen. Forecasts must have clearly defined terms and timelines. They must use numbers and we need a lot of them since we cannot judge one probabilistic forecast.

After the five years had elapsed, who had most often made the correct predictions and which category seemed to have made the most mistakes? Tetlock was unable to find any relationship between his categories and the accuracy of the predictions – except for one:

The one and only reliable factor was the distinction between what he classified as *hedgehogs* and *foxes*, based on the archetypes of Sir Isaiah Berlin.[30] Hedgehogs are 'big idea' thinkers, who love grand theories. They have one dominant vision, are very self-confident and know how to win an argument by multiplying reasons why they are right and others are wrong. Foxes, however, are more eclectic and flexible in their ideas. And because they avoid over-simplification, they make fewer errors.

Tetlock found that – on average – the hedgehogs scored low on their predictions. The thinking of hedgehogs is dominated by a single idea, which they constantly apply to every domain and every new situation. They force the explanatory value of that one idea onto the interpretation of each new one. They want to push square pegs into round holes.

On average, the foxes, on the other hand, scored very well with their predictions. Foxes are sceptical about obvious historical analogies. They base their arguments on probabilities and they adjust their models easily when there are new facts or data.

What is important, Tetlock concluded, is the way the foxes gathered their knowledge and kept it up to date: the wider their curiosity and interest (the context!), the more accurate and correct their predictions. The hedgehogs remained locked in their initial idea, because they wanted to understand it fully. This is a fatal mistake in a complex world that is constantly changing!

One final finding of Tetlock perhaps gives an answer to the question we posed at the beginning of this chapter: how were things able to go so terribly wrong in Iraq? Tetlock's results showed that when hedgehogs are wrong in their predictions, they are usually completely and entirely wrong.

It is not easy to think like a fox, but a broad curiosity about changes in the environment and an ability to keep knowledge up to date are of great importance. As Tetlock demonstrates, insight into underlying relationships and systems and a continual search for new ideas are important factors for making good predictions and adjusting to new situations.

## About 'believers' and 'non-believers'

Do you think, at this point, that a method of future thinking is a better tool to prepare for the future? Are you sceptical about a combined academic and arts-based method? Do you not believe in a method that enables better anticipation of future uncertainties, complex problems and rapid changes? Another possibility is that you simply do not know whether you should believe it or not. Or perhaps you think it is nonsense and have rejected it already.

In fact, one can form an attitude in many different ways about new concepts and information, and not just about future thinking. However, recognizing your own attitude and that of others is extremely important for future thinking in particular. And this is certainly the case when dealing with wicked problems.

To clarify what we mean, let us take a look at the context within which our future generations of leaders are preparing to make their decisions: our universities and colleges. Consider the following story of a professor who sets his students an exam assignment.

The professor has completed his course and has discussed the new concepts it contains with the students. He now needs to test whether the students have understood the concepts and know how to apply them. The professor does this by asking clear questions that offer verifiable answers. In short, the right background information has been given in advance, the questions have been clearly formulated, there is a clear distinction between right and wrong answers and there is plenty of time to complete the exam paper.

What a difference with the problems facing decision-makers in the real worlds of business, defence or politics! In those contexts, problems are not presented on a silver platter, as they are in an academic or pedagogic context.

Research published in 1983 by Donald Schön shows that the relevant practical problems or challenges we are facing do not have academic solutions in a majority of the cases. In fact, he concludes that academic solutions to practical problems are rare.

First of all, in the real world the problem – and therefore the right question – is often unclear. In these circumstances, there is no point in having ready-made models and theories that you can use to solve the problem before you even know what the problem is! Decision-makers are faced with important decisions involving different type of problems, most notably wicked problems. This type of problem does not have a defined domain. To believe that you can collect and process all the relevant information is therefore an illusion. Usually, there is not enough time to thoroughly complete all the analyses – because by then the context will have already changed. Finally, the formulated answers are rarely verifiable: the controversy as to whether this, that or no decision was the right one will therefore continue.

How, then, do decision-makers work? As they did in the past, when there was insufficient information available: on the basis of their best judgment, intuition, conjecture, experience in similar situations, observations, anecdotes, metaphors and analogies. In other words, in a pragmatic, ad-hoc manner. There is nothing wrong with pragmatism: many pragmatic decision-makers have made good decisions.

But how do these practical decision-makers view concepts when it is not clear whether or not they can be applied to a particular problem? Or how do they assess new information that is often incomplete, not always relevant or arrives too late?

It is important as a decision-maker to be aware of your attitude towards new concepts and new information. It is also tremendously important to know and understand how others think, especially if you need to work together. In addition, you cannot ignore reflecting on the following question: to what extent do you believe in the correctness of the available information? This is especially important for information about the future. It is not enough simply to state whether or not you agree, because these questions are too complex.

An important contribution in thinking on these matters was made by Herman Kahn. His approach was as original as it was relevant: because such questions are often a matter of faith, he looked at the concepts of religion and law.

In religion, the different gradations of faith (which is certainly based on uncertain information!) have long been studied, while in law courts judges and jury members rule on guilt or innocence on the basis of evidence that is sometimes convincing, sometimes unreliable but always incomplete. What can we learn from this?

Kahn sets six gradations of belief that can be applied to a theory, a proposition, a concept or a policy, as shown in Figure 3:

**Figure 3: The six degrees of belief in new concepts and information**

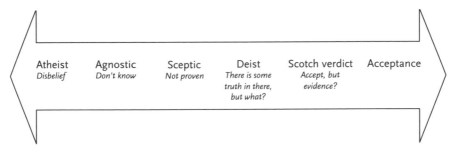

*Source:* based on Kahn H. (1979) The Agnostic Use of Information and Concepts, in Aligica P. D., Weinstein K. R., Eds. (2009) The Essential, Herman Kahn, pp. 167-176.

An *atheistic* attitude towards new concepts and information means more or less total disbelief and rejection. Someone who does not know whether or not the new concept or information is credible takes an *agnostic* position. The *sceptic* in this context is someone who is willing to believe, but has doubts and would therefore like to see more data, arguments or evidence. The *deist* accepts that there is some merit in the idea, but is not sure of the specific details or the extent of the validity.

The *Scotch verdict* is something special. The term refers to a specificity of the Scottish legal system, which leaves room for a sentence without a decision. In Scottish criminal law, the jury must not choose exclusively between guilty or innocent; there is also a third possibility: the verdict of 'not proven'. A case against a defendant might be very convincing, while the burden of proof still does not meet the statutory provision of 'beyond reasonable doubt'. In our context, 'not proven' can therefore be understood to mean 'almost proven' or 'the proof is good enough for me'.

This is the most important of Kahn's six attitudes, because it is highly relevant when there are difficult decisions to be made: we have information that we consider to be sufficiently valid for a policy decision or an individual choice to be made, but this is still very different from applying rigorous academic or mathematical standards of proof. The vast majority of decisions falls into this category: good enough for the person or group concerned, taken seriously, but impossible to be proved scientifically.

*Acceptance* does not automatically imply that the new concept or information is true. It just means that the person or group concerned has no reason or desire to question the new concept or information at this stage. This is often the case when the concept or information conforms to the values, ideology or even the prejudices of the group. Acceptance is often unnoticed, because it is so self-evident, so immediate and so widely shared.

In other words, when faced with future thinking, we can have a variety of approaches, ranging from atheistic rejection to immediate acceptance. We must remember, however, that the available information and/or proof at our disposal is likely to be insufficient, because we are dealing with the future. For this reason, both extremes are particularly dangerous when it comes to future thinking. Atheistic rejection clings to a fixed vision and ignores new signals (this is the attitude of Tetlock's hedgehogs), while blind acceptance fails to question anything. An agnostic attitude allows us to be receptive to signals but postpones making a decision, so that progress cannot be made. The best position is perhaps the *Scotch verdict*: we take decisions as before, but do not condemn concepts and information about the future. On the contrary, we keep different options open and we organize ourselves to collect more proof – by snuffling like Tetlock's foxes!

In the next chapter we will investigate how we can examine and interpret this context in a methodical way.

## Summary

1. Keith Grint characterized problems based on the characteristics of the environment in which the problem is situated. He distinguished:

   - A critical problem: a crisis that demands an instant response (by a commander).
   - A tamed problem: a problem where the context is more complex in comparison with a critical problem. There are existing processes that can be used to manage this type of problem and the solution lies in implementing the process correctly (by a process-manager).
   - A wicked problem: a problem that arises in an environment where uncertainty is great, where change is rapid and where complexity is increasing. The approach requires leadership. It is essential for leaders operating in such an environment not only to ask the right questions but also to seek the cooperation of others, because the interpretation of the (future) environment is critical (by a leader).

2. When does future thinking offer a better method?

   - When problems are highly complex and difficult to define.
   - When testing strategic options.
   - When anticipating new events.
   - When developing innovations and new options.
   - When identifying uncertainties and risks.
   - When the future orientation of a group, organization, region or country is at stake.
   - When forming a vision and creating a better world.

3. Our cultural background influences the way we interpret the environment. Asians look for changes in the environment more than Westerners, who prefer to focus on their objective and pay less attention to the interpretation of the changing context.

4. To improve our interpretation of the (future) environment or context, we need to be sceptical about obvious historical analogies. Instead, we must reason in terms of possible and probable future developments, rather than in terms of a single, dominant, officially sanctioned idea of the future. Like snuffling foxes,

we must widen our interest and curiosity for a broader social and international environment and must develop a second nature to detect new ideas and concepts. Hedgehogs, on the other hand, cling too stubbornly to the dominant idea, which they push forward as an explanation for all problems. This limited view of an excessively narrow (business) environment lacks flexibility and can lead to catastrophic decisions in a complex and changing world.

5. Many attitudes are possible towards future thinking and towards new concepts and new information in general. These attitudes range from atheistic rejection to immediate acceptance. They are particularly useful when dealing with the future, where information and proof are, by definition, insufficient. However, the extremes of atheism and acceptance are both pernicious to future thinking: the former continues to adhere to a single and incontestable vision that ignores new signals, while the latter questions nothing. An agnostic attitude allows new signals to be received, but leaves the decision in the middle, so that no progress can be made. The best attitude is that of the *Scotch verdict*: decisions are taken as before, but without rejecting possible concepts or information about the future. On the contrary, all options are kept open, while new efforts are made to collect and interpret relevant information.

# Chapter 3
# No future without method

*"We cannot solve problems by using the same kind of thinking we used when we created them."*
Albert Einstein (1879-1955)

Future thinking: what does this approach embrace? In this chapter we will answer this question and point out its importance in today's world. To understand the benefits and full richness of future thinking, we will look at two important aspects in more depth: the difference between uncertainty and predictability on the one hand and the precise purpose of a future project on the other hand.

*The working group of the pharmaceutical company from the previous chapter handed their proposals as agreed to the next meeting of the board of directors. The first sentence was: "The environment in which the company has been successful for years is profoundly changing." The working group advised the board to map out these changes in the environment and to assess their possible and probable future evolutions. Only then would it be feasible to examine how these changes had altered the business model and strategy that had made the company so successful in the past: a combination of world-class research with commercial excellence. This would help them to find the right approach to the most crucial question of all: should the strategy be renewed and, if so, how?*

*The working group concluded that the company first needed a new approach to read and understand the future environment, so that it could anticipate future changes and problems. In short, the organization needed to learn what was happening in the environment – and it needed to learn it better and more quickly. The last sentence of the working group's review reads as follows: "We face a wicked problem and the appropriate method to deal with this kind of problem is future thinking. If we want to become a company that can create the future again, we must first and foremost learn to understand this method of future thinking from A to Z."*

## What is future thinking?

The success of an organization in the future does not depend on the study of the future, but of the future success of decisions that are taken in the present. The leaders of society – entrepreneurs, administrators, social and political leaders – have been faced with many discontinuous and disruptive changes during the past few years and this is unlikely to change in the immediate future. The banking sector worldwide was surprised by what happened in 2008. International groups such as AIG, Merrill Lynch, Goldman Sachs, Lehman Brothers and Bear Stearns almost (or in some cases completely) went to the wall.[31] The car industry was also confronted with major and unforeseen difficulties (*e.g.* GM, Opel, Saab and Volvo). From 2011 onwards, even a number of countries *suddenly and unexpectedly* found themselves with serious problems: first Greece, then later Italy, Portugal, and Spain (the so-called PIGS). And these were not the only countries that struggled (and continue to struggle) with membership of the euro zone. In times of great uncertainty, organizations must evaluate their vision of the future more thoroughly than ever: how can they prepare for the future by anticipating more and making better plans?

What methods are used in practice to reflect in a systematic way on the future? Four groups can be identified:

- *Forecasting*: making predictions based on current information to ensure a surprise-free future. The methods used are extrapolation and trends analysis. The analysis goes from the past to the future.
- *Foresight*: anticipating the consequences of a number of different possible futures. This is often done with strategic scenarios. The analysis goes from the present to the future.
- *Backcasting*: this method defines a desirable future and then looks at the strategy needed from the present onwards to create this future.
- *Critical futures*: these are futures defined on the basis of the prescriptive norms today. These are often political futures used in social or political debates: "What we do should be based on what we believe."

In practice, one often finds a combination of these methods. For each individual method, there is also a combination of qualitative or quantitative tools that can be used (*cf.* Figure 9 and Table 4).

In times when organizations are confronted with huge turbulence and uncertainty, they must check and evaluate their vision and their assumptions about the future more rigorously than ever before, critically reviewing their planning systems time after time after time! However, the problem with the traditional forms of future exploration found in business and strategic plans of almost all of today's companies is that these plans, as well as their corresponding investments and strategies, are based on *forecasts*. These are predictions based on past trends or on plans that are believed to be the *most likely* to develop in the future. This method is very well adapted to ensure a surprise-free future and it is a method used at the highest levels of government. For example, forecasts based on assumptions made typically by a central planning bureau or a bureau for economic policy analysis, using extrapolations from econometric models, are frequently used for state budget calculations.

Unfortunately, research has shown time and time again that organizations planning for just one 'probable' future will sooner or later be surprised, confused and left behind, once they are faced with a different kind of future. Worse still, they are at an added disadvantage when the external factors are unfavourable, for which – as a result of their focus on that one probable future – they are totally unprepared. To add insult to injury, the research has also shown that this so-called 'unforeseen future' is in many cases not quite as unforeseeable as you might think.

Often it is enough to proactively take a range of possible futures into account. In this way, there is a good chance that you will anticipate – in part, at least, – the reality that ultimately comes to pass. This means that you will be prepared and will have an essential strategic advantage over your less forward-thinking rivals. The possible consequences of failing to look sufficiently ahead can be read, for example, in the report (published on 23 July 2012) of the Investigation Committee into the nuclear accident at the Fukushima nuclear power plant of the Tokyo Electric Power Company (TEPCO):

> *"The government and TEPCO failed to prevent the disaster not because a large tsunami was unanticipated, but because they were reluctant to invest time, effort and money in protecting against a natural disaster they considered to be unlikely."*

Whoever wants to fully make use of the benefits of future thinking must prepare their organization thoroughly. On the one hand, this means introducing the methods that make it possible to learn from the future. On the other hand, it means linking this approach to the methods and processes of decision-making based on the principles of strategic management. We define this process and the accompanying culture that makes it possible by the term *strategic conversations*. It is a culture that enables an organization to cope with facts and uncertainty, as well as lack of knowledge and understanding, and ignorance. The essence of these ideas is to be found in Nassim Nicholas Taleb's 2001 book *Fooled by Randomness*, which was well summarized by the 21st U.S. Secretary of Defence, Donald H. Rumsfeld, at a press conference[32] at NATO Headquarters in Brussels on 6 June 2002:

> *"The message is that there are no "knowns." There are things we know that we know. There are known unknowns. That is to say there are things that we now know we don't know. But there are also unknown unknowns. There are things we don't know we don't know. So when we do the best we can and we pull all this information together, and we then say, well that's basically what we see as the situation, that is really only the known knowns and the known unknowns. And each year, we discover a few more of those unknown unknowns."*

The strategic conversation is fuelled by a process of strategic scenario planning or scenario-based thinking, together with an extended form of *horizon scanning*. Both are followed by a measurement system that promotes the early detection of fundamental changes in the environment and develops hypotheses on the basis of whichever future will unfold (*EWS: early warning systems*). The combination of these processes arms an organization much better than the traditional processes – which only deal with one unique 'official' future – for success in the future, and so it helps to maintain competitive position in the present.

Scenario-based thinking is therefore a key element in this future thinking approach. The word 'scenario' is derived from the ancient Greek word *skènè* (Σκηνη), which means 'drama'. A scenario can be defined as a chronological description of a particular event or series of events that have taken place or have yet to take place. Scenarios form a coherent set of assumptions that provide the basis for future projections. A future projection is a description of possible and plausible futures, grounded with logical steps.

With the scenario method, we can describe plausible alternative future projections for a specific part of the future. Scenarios are developed and investigated methodologically in groups of two, three, four or more different coherent futures. They are used to study the impact of these different futures on organizations or the decisions of organizations.

## Limitations to learning from the future

However, our vision of the future is limited on two different levels: on the one hand, we do not have complete information, notwithstanding all our efforts to collect data and information; on the other hand, our imagination limits our capacity to understand, interpret and make correlations. In other words, our ability to develop a vision for the future is limited by both our ignorance and our imagination.

Scenarios are a method to help the leaders of society to structure their know-how, their knowledge and their creativity (what they can depict) into logical and useful evolutions of possible futures. In this way, the impact of these *alternative futures* on their current and future strategic choices can be examined in a systematic and structured way.

Scenarios are therefore a combination of estimating of what could happen and making assumptions about what might happen: both a science and an art.

## What the scenario method is not

Scenarios are not predictions about what will happen, nor are they extrapolations from the past (forecasts)! The scenario method is not a method to improve our predictive powers! Projections, forecasts and predictions are three different things:

- *Forecast*: is an estimation of a future situation in advance, based on expertise, systems or calculations (statistics and regression analysis).
- *Projection*: is a certain vision of the future, based on specific information and on a collection of logical assumptions.
- *Prediction*: is a statement about the future.

Before we go any further, we would like to point out yet another important distinction: uncertainty in this context should not be confused with improbability, unpredictability or risk.

## Uncertainty vs. Predictability vs. Risk

Figure 4 illustrates graphically the relationship between the following elements:

- *Predictability*: is a quantitative measure of the possible likelihood that an event will occur. It therefore requires a probability distribution that measures the chance a future occurrence will happen, based on statistical data collected from identical historical events.
- *Uncertainty*: is when we do not know what problems, trends, decisions or events will shape the future. Uncertainty does not imply that we do not know what the future will be; it just means that we do not know what trends and driving forces will be important.

Predictability decreases when a future event depends on circumstances that we cannot estimate or anticipate. The outcome is then uncertain. Dealing with this uncertainty is not a question of finding a probability, because no probability can be linked to this. So how can you deal with uncertainty is this situation? A good technique is to prepare an agenda of possible problems or issues. This is a list of the uncertainties that managers think are important for the future of their organization.

Several possible futures will need to be worked out in scenarios. These scenarios are all equally possible or plausible! Given the considerable uncertainty surrounding the future, with its ever increasing complexity and changes, the value of scenario-based thinking is that it offers greater insight into *possible* evolutions. In this way, you can estimate here and now what the possible consequences of decisions made today (or even later) will be in the different future scenarios. Future thinking is situated in the space where uncertainty increases and predictability decreases (grey area – Figure 4). The speed at which this happens depends on the level of turbulence in the environment.

Does this mean that future thinking is a recipe for dealing with all future uncertainties and that each organization should henceforth ban forecasts, marketing reports and econometric models? Certainly not!

**Figure 4: The relationship between predictability and uncertainty**

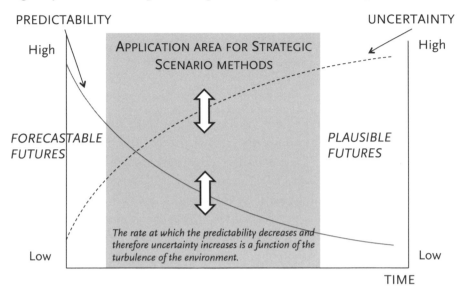

PREDICTABILITY                                                    UNCERTAINTY

High                    APPLICATION AREA FOR STRATEGIC        High
                         SCENARIO METHODS

FORECASTABLE                                              PLAUSIBLE
FUTURES                                                   FUTURES

                 *The rate at which the predictability decreases and*
                 *therefore uncertainty increases is a function of the*
Low              *turbulence of the environment.*                    Low

                                                              TIME

*Source*: based on van der Heijden K. (2005).

Forecasts and strategic or future scenarios need to be applied together in a sensible way, although awareness of the limitations of existing forecasting methods needs to be taken into account, as Figure 4 clearly shows. Having said this, predictions are often the basis for the trend analysis that lies at the heart of good strategic conversations. Unfortunately, managers often fail to use scenarios because they confuse them with extrapolations, which often have a poor reputation. Extrapolations are certainly unreliable when it comes to predicting the unpredictable or the uncertain.

There is also a deeper reason why future thinking is so rare: this is connected with the role played by managers. A process of scenario development and strategic conversations requires an open mind and the active participation of senior management, including full knowledge of all relevant details – without this knowledge, no strategic conversation is possible. For a weak manager, this may sound threatening. In Chapter 4, we will address this theme in more depth, discussing new forms of leadership for turbulent environments.

Finally, it is important to stress that *risk* is not the same as *uncertainty*.[33] This distinction was first articulated from an economic perspective by Frank Hyneman Knight (1885-1972).[34] He was an economist by training, a philosopher and historian by inclination and a professor at the University of Chicago, where he played a key role in the early development of the so-called *Chicago School of Economics*.[35] He is perhaps most well-known for his famous statement: *"You cannot be certain about uncertainty"*. Based on his award-winning doctoral thesis written in 1921, his seminal work is *Risk, Uncertainty and Profit*.[36] In it, he describes the difference between risk and uncertainty as follows:

> *"Uncertainty must be taken in a sense radically distinct from the familiar notion of risk, from which it has never been properly separated... The essential fact is that 'risk' means in some cases a quantity susceptible of measurement, while at other times it is something distinctly not of this character; and there are far-reaching and crucial differences in the bearings of the phenomena depending on which of the two is really present and operating... It will appear that a measurable uncertainty, or 'risk' proper, as we shall use the term, is so far different from an unmeasurable one that it is not in effect an uncertainty at all."*

Frank Knight devised a simple experiment that allows for a clearer understanding of the difference between *forecast, risk* and *uncertainty*. Such an understanding is crucial, since all three concepts are very important and can be found in the everyday environment of decision-makers. The experiment goes as follows:

In a classroom filled with students there are three big bowls. The first bowl is transparent, the other two are opaque. The first bowl is filled with sweets, half of which are wrapped in brown wrapping paper and the other half in a yellow wrapper. The second jar is also filled with sweets, but with different wrapping paper: half in red and the remaining half in blue. Finally, the third bowl is filled, but this time with a variety of small objects: pens, sweets, a small clock, a small piece of chocolate, a key chain, *etc.*

The first transparent bowl is shown to a student and he is asked to predict the first thing he will pull out of the bowl. If the student guesses correctly, he can keep the article (*i.e.* eat the sweet). Otherwise, he must place it back in the bowl.

What happens next? The student pulls something from the first bowl and checks the result. This is repeated two or three times. The smart students quickly realize that the result is predictable. The same sweets keep appearing and the only difference is the wrapping paper, which is either brown or yellow. From then on, the guessing is quickly done – and so is the eating of the sweets!

The experiment moves on to the second opaque bowl. A sweet wrapped in red paper is drawn, which is initially a surprise. But after pulling two or three more sweets, the students realize what is going on. They are soon convinced that the second bowl also contains sweets, but this time wrapped in red and blue paper.

The experiment now comes to the final bowl. The students once again expect again to find sweets, but this time they are a bit more cautious. After all, university professors do not usually conduct such simple experiments during their lectures! The first draw from the third bowl is indeed a surprise: it is a pen! Are there no sweets anymore? But an even bigger surprise is yet to come: after a few more draws, it is clear that there is no longer any relationship with the previous two bowls. This starts a lively discussion among the students about what possible theories can predict the next draw, but none of them hold water, because every theory is contradicted by the following draw. It soon becomes apparent that it is impossible to predict what will come out of the third bowl.

## So what can we learn from this experiment?

The first bowl corresponds to what we call a *forecast* or predictability: we know the probability distribution, which allows us to calculate or predict in advance – *ex ante* – the chance that an event will occur. This is also what happens in games of chance, such as playing the lottery or going to a casino.

The second bowl corresponds to *risk*. We know in advance – *a priori* – the probability distribution. Taking samples allows us to estimate what the theoretical probability distribution might be. This is also what insurance companies and proficient bankers do.

The third bowl corresponds to *Knightian uncertainty*. We do not know the nature of the objects in the bowl and every prediction is therefore impossible. This is the field where innovative entrepreneurs, diplomats, political leaders and military commanders are active, dealing with new markets, new geopolitical shocks or new types of warfare. They all are confronted with *black swans*.[37]

These are useful conclusions in their own right. However, a critical and analytical mind can get much more out of this experiment.

Firstly, the uncertainty in the third bowl is not so high that we can say nothing meaningful about the objects. They must be small, otherwise they would not fit into the bowl. What's more, one bright student shook the bowl before making his draw and it made noise, so that we know the objects must also be hard. In other words, we can still say something about the contents of the bowl within certain limits. We can therefore speak of the *cone of uncertainty*. This means that we know within certain limits the boundaries of the uncertainty.

A second comment relates to the second bowl, the first opaque one. The students concluded after only a few draws that this bowl also contained sweets and that they were wrapped equally in red and blue paper. In fact, however, there was no guarantee that this was the case for all the sweets in the bowl. The conclusion of the students should therefore not have been *"The second bowl contains only red and blue wrapped candies"* but: *"The second bowl contains, among others, red and blue wrapped candies."*[38]

Of course, at the bottom of the second bowl, deep under all sweets, we have put a marble! At the end of the experiment, this marble will inevitably be pulled out, resulting in surprise and incomprehension! The students have just experienced a *black swan*!

Dealing with risks seems so familiar to us that we think we know everything about them once we understand the relevant statistical distributions. In fact, risks are a special case of an uncertain environment, in which the black swan has not yet appeared.

Knight's simple experiment improves our understanding of the nature and behaviour of the environment. Situations where we have advanced knowledge of the probability distribution are extremely rare and roughly correspond to forms of gambling. A situation in which the probability distribution is estimated on the basis of historical data is much more dangerous: we can assume for far too long that everything is known and under control, until a black swan or a strategic shock occurs to shake us awake. In practice, however, most environments are characterized by uncertainty and turbulence, although that is not always immediately obvious. It is in this kind of uncertain environment that political leaders, entrepreneurs, military commanders and business leaders take most of their decisions. Models and extrapolations based on historical data should therefore only be used with caution and knowledge.

## Complexity: an introduction[39]

Every day our world becomes more complex and dynamic. Global population continues to rise, with urbanization increasing at an exponential rate. Economic growth brings people from diverse cultures and regions into contact with one another through increased trade, travel and migration. The internet and social media now seem to connect everyone with everyone else and make a wealth of information freely available to all.

In many ways, this accelerating interconnectedness has made life better. But it has also brought greater complexity to world affairs. Many of the grand challenges that confront humanity – problems as diverse as climate change, the stability of markets, the availability of energy and resources, poverty and conflict – often seem to entail impenetrable webs of cause and effect.

But these problems are not necessarily as impenetrable as they might seem. Powerful new tools have given scientists a better understanding of complexity. Instead of looking at a system in isolation, complexity scientists step back and look at how the many different parts interact to form a coherent whole. Whatever the object of study happens to be, complexity scientists assemble data, search for patterns and regularities, and build models to understand the dynamics and organization of the system. They step back from the parts and look at the whole.

This kind of thinking is a major departure from traditional science. For centuries, scientists have worked by reducing the object of study down to its constituent components. Complexity science, by contrast, provides a complementary perspective by seeking to understand systems as interacting elements that form, change, and evolve over time.

The multiplicity of ideas, concepts, techniques and approaches embodied by the science of complexity can be applied to people, organizations and society as a whole, from economies and companies to epidemics and the environment.

## The science of complexity: new tools for new perspectives

Complexity is not so much a subject of research as a new way of looking at phenomena. It is inherently interdisciplinary, meaning that it derives its problems from the real world and its concepts and methods from all fields of science. Complexity lies at the root of the most burning issues that face us every day, such as hunger, energy, water, health, climate, security, urbanization, sustainability, innovation and the impact of technology.

To get a feeling for how complexity science can work in the real world, consider the very concrete problem of automobile traffic. The vehicle through-rate of a highway rises as the density of motor vehicles increases, and at a critical point a traffic jam forms. The jam can disappear and reappear over time, or slowly move up or down the highway. Over the network of roads that form the wider metropolitan area, traffic jams appear, disappear and reappear – not randomly, but in patterns, such as a series of waves.

Complex systems by their very nature resist simple examples, but for the sake of clarity our traffic example can illustrate some of the characteristics of complex systems. At the heart is a collection of objects or agents (cars, in this case) that compete for some kind of limited resource, such as food, space, power, energy or wealth (roads, in this example). The complexity of the problem lies in the large number of interactions between these agents. From many individual interactions, new and often surprising phenomena emerge (waves of traffic jams). The emergent behaviour of the whole cannot be reduced to the individual agents of the system: the whole is more than the sum of its parts.

All complex systems exist within their own environment and are part of that environment. As the environment changes, so they adapt. Traffic is not merely a question of the number and speed of cars but is also affected by the number of existing roads, traffic lights and potholes. Change these components and traffic patterns change – the agents adapt to their environment. In this sense, the system and its environment co-evolve. The agents are connected to one another (drivers see the tail lights of the car in front of them). They are interconnected, which means they can interact.

Most other real-world phenomena have these same key qualities. An influenza outbreak involves a complex interplay of people, viruses and an environment that includes plane travel, health care and social mixing. The interaction of financial instruments, banks and investor psychology makes for a complex financial system that fluctuates constantly, most of the time in small degrees but every once in a while with a crash. Ideas and social norms – acceptance of gay marriage, say, or market-driven socialism – can propagate through society according to the principles of complex systems.

Working to resolve or influence many of the most important issues that society faces requires a basic understanding of complexity, not least because complex systems have a propensity to make sudden, unpredictable and drastic changes.

## Governance and non-linearity

Scientific knowledge is organized in departments by disciplines (physics, engineering, economics, biology, sociology). Government agencies are organized in departments by policy issues (food, health, international trade, human rights). Public and private institutes frequently follow that same framework. The trouble is that all the world's prominent challenges are essentially non-disciplinary and transcend the policy of particular departments.

When competition for water triggers war and disease is the aftermath, no government agency or NGO is set up to see the whole picture. This mismatch stands in the way of understanding the real nature of the grand challenges we face and in taking appropriate action in response to a crisis. It also stands in the way of finding sustainable approaches to meeting our challenges.

One of the most dangerous assumptions in world governance, and in the sciences for that matter, is the assumption of linearity. Linearity basically means that each effect has a single cause, and that the cause and effect are proportional to one another. In a complex system, there are feedback loops and cycles that make emergent behaviour unpredictable. Negative feedback can act to keep a condition stable, but it can also be destabilizing. So can positive feedback, or self-amplification. The 'flash crash' of 2010, in which the NYSE Dow Jones Index dropped 10% in the span of a few minutes, was one such non-linearity caused by negative feedback, in this case computer trading. The revolution in Tunisia and across the Arab world was a non-linear (disproportionate) response to the action (self-immolation) of a single street vendor. The failure of Lehman Brothers triggered a totally disproportionate collapse of the global financial system.

## Reductionism

Most present-day leaders have been trained to assume that the world behaves according to simple rules. This mind-set reduces complex facts, entities, phenomena or structures to some simple notion. Reductionism totally ignores the phenomenon of emergence; *i.e.* the fact that the whole has properties that cannot be reduced to the properties of the parts. As complexity scientist John Holland notes:

> *"For the last 400 years science has advanced by reductionism. The idea is that you could understand the world, all of nature, by examining smaller and smaller pieces of it. When assembled, the small pieces would explain the whole".*

The grand challenges or problems we are facing cannot be solved through a reductionist approach. Complexity thinking and science help us to build bridges between different specialties and disciplines. It can help us to understand dynamic, highly interconnected and interdependent systems, where traditional sciences fail.

## Applications

Complexity science is not an applied science as such; but it is a science that leads to insights or understandings that have been applied to real-world problems. Some of these applications have major implications for the governance of corporations, regional, national and international institutions, as well as social and ecological systems; perhaps more so than ever before, given the increasing availability of 'big data' about our techno-socio-economic-environmental systems.

Here are some of the issues to which insights from complexity science have been applied: combating HIV, military strategy, designing and using economic incentives, designing for resilience, using scarce resources more efficiently, software development, language acquisition, avoiding conflicts and crises or mitigating their severity or consequences.

These problems are interconnected, some of them strongly. Complexity science already has a variety of tools and methods that can help to address these problems, or at least have the potential to do so. Combining social and complexity sciences has also led to a number of interesting applications, including models for self-organization and segregation (which suggest strategies to reduce crime and conflict), models for social cooperation (which involve ways of overcoming the so-called tragedies of the commons), and models for the formation of opinions (which are used as prediction tools in the market).

Models of pedestrian dynamics can now help to anticipate and avoid crowd disasters. Models of mobility patterns and traffic breakdowns support congestion avoidance and inform the design of smarter cities. Models of financial systems offer suggestions on how to make these systems more stable and resilient to shocks.

Simulations of supply chains facilitate more efficient production systems and provide a better understanding of business cycles. Models of conflict and organized crime hold the promise to reduce wars, insurgency, and drug traffic. Real-time measurement and simulation of pandemics can be used for scenario-based policy recommendations; for example, regarding more effective immunization strategies.

## Complexity, data and social systems

Obtaining data about social interactions used to be very time consuming and cumbersome. Lately, this has been simplified dramatically by new surveying methods and by the internet. Due to digitization, data are available abundantly on many issues that were not measured nor effectively measurable before digitization spread. The enormous volume of data that is becoming available as a result is known as 'big data'.

Parallel to this data explosion, much progress has been made in modelling the key elements of social systems. Examples include the previously mentioned models for the emergence of cooperation in social dilemma situations (which normally promote a 'tragedy of the commons'), the formation of social norms, preventing the spread of conflicts or violence, and the promotion of collective behaviour (in fields such as opinion formation, crowd disasters and revolutions). Currently, scientists are working on models that consider emotions, models that explain the preconditions for altruism, and models that examine cognitive complexity. It is expected that using big data to calibrate and validate such models will enable many beneficial applications for society to be developed. Complexity science is quickly gaining in practical importance.

Generic characteristics of complex systems

- Self-organization
- Interdependence
- Feedback
- Far from equilibrium
- Exploration of the space of possibilities
- History and path dependence
- Creation of new order

Major issues related to complexity

- Spread of epidemics
- Climate change
- Escalating conflicts
- Governance of increasingly complex social systems
- Potential collapses or shifts in ecosystems
- Cascading failures; for example, in electricity networks
- Irrational effects of financial speculation
- Networks of terrorists
- Diffusion of fashions, innovations and the spread of rumours
- Self-organizing mass movements; for example, the London riots, the Arab Spring

This list can be extended almost endlessly.

It is only through intense interdisciplinary collaboration that it will be possible to discover and understand the underlying principles that govern the complexity of our world. And it is only through such an understanding that we can hope to successfully deal with the grand challenges that we face in the decades ahead. *"The nations and people who master the new sciences of complexity will become the economic, cultural and political superpowers of the twenty-first century,"* said physicist Heinz R. Pagels (1939-1988). His words were more recently echoed by the world-renowned physicist and cosmologist, Stephen W. Hawking FRS, when he declared: *"The twenty-first century will be the century of complexity."*

## What is the purpose of a future project?

A future project, as the name implies, is intended to contribute to the future development of an organization. Depending on the objective and the time frame, it is possible in broad terms to distinguish four different approaches. A good definition of the objective of the future project is important, because only then can the adequate approach be selected:

- Is the future project aimed at the development and survival of an organization? We will look at this form in more depth shortly.
- Does the future project relate to a crisis situation and is the project embedded into a crisis management approach? If so, the main objective will be to improve the systems or to design behavioural training (for example, the type of training that uses flight simulators for pilots in critical situations).
- Is the future project concerned with the scientific world? If so, the main objective will be to improve communication between different disciplines for the development of scientific theories and models (for example, on the theme of climate change).
- Finally, there is a fourth category of future project for the formulation of political policy. Here, the main objective is to involve all stakeholders in policy decisions and/or implementation. Later, we will discuss an example from this category using the *Mont Fleur* scenarios, which reflect a historic moment in the evolution of South Africa.

Whatever the objective, future thinking ultimately always serves as a test bed for the critical trial of a policy or strategy. In environments with high uncertainty, it is essential to know how *robust* the chosen strategy is likely to be when subjected to unforeseen shocks. Even though a project may initially start with the limited intention of better understanding a confused environment, sooner or later there will be need (and a desire) to test decisions in various (future) environments. Or as Arie de Geus observed: *"Future is plural"*. Consequently, you always need to keep the strategically important domain you want to test in mind. This means that the first task of an intelligent strategist is to define *the objective* of the project with precision!

In the following paragraphs, we will discuss in more detail the first of the above mentioned categories: how to define the objectives of projects aimed at developing, restructuring or turning around large organizations.

## The objective when attempting to expand an organization

How do you document the objectives of a future project? An important question that needs to be answered in order to define the objective is: *"Why are we doing this scenario project?"* Two further questions can be helpful in this respect:

- Is it a *one-off project* or is strategic future thinking part of a *continuous process* within the organization? A one-off project aims to tackle a specific point of discussion. The objective of a continuous process is to build competencies for future thinking throughout the organization. This makes a world of difference!
- Is the major benefit of the future project expected to promote new perspectives, so that new questions can be defined properly? Or it is also expected that the project will provide answers or will contribute to the *decision-making* process?

We can combine these two questions to create a target matrix (Table 2).

### Table 2: The target matrix

|  | One-off project | Continuous process |
|---|---|---|
| **New perspectives** | • A one-off exploration project to identify key questions. <br> • For an organization that has ended up in rough waters and has difficulties identifying what the environment desires from it. Main objective: *sensemaking (interpreting)* | • A continuous exploration activity. <br> • For organizations that have too often made wrong assessments in the past relating to developments and changes in the environment. The entire organization must therefore be constantly retuned to better identify relevant issues and questions in a sustained strategic conversation. <br> • Main objective: *building anticipation competence* |
| **Decision-making** | • A one-off scenario project to make decisions. <br> • For organizations that need to take a key decision, where the level of uncertainty is so high that the decision-making process is more difficult. <br> • Main objective : *strategic specification* | • A continuous decision-making process. <br> • For organizations that operate in very rapidly changing environments or work in sectors where regularly 'all-or-nothing' decisions need to be taken about the allocation of huge company assets. The main task here is to investigate, observe and understand. Based on this, the aim is to build a competitive advantage in critical decision-making processes. <br> • Main objective: *building a learning organization* |

*Source:* based on van der Heijden K. (2005), p.161.

The matrix also provides a hierarchy of objectives: specific future projects (for example, to understand the environment better, as in the top-left corner or to determine strategy, as in the bottom-left corner) are steps that can only truly lead to competitive advantage when the necessary competences are built. In other words, when we move to the right side of the matrix.

The ultimate goal is to create a *learning organization*.[40] In practice, the first step is to start from a specific project, but in order to succeed this project must have a limited objective, such as:

- Understanding and interpreting the environment
- Exploration
- Testing strategy
- Anticipating and detecting weak signals
- Generating unique insights

Examples of objectives to create a learning organization are:

- Turning tacit knowledge into sharable knowledge
- Building consensus
- Initiating and encouraging strategic conversations
- Team building
- Building a unique spirit and morale
- Communicating difficult messages

Now that we have explained the importance of first defining in clear and explicit terms the objective of a scenario exercise, we can address the next key question: *"How do you tackle a planning scenario project?"* We will deal with this question in Chapter 5. Before that, we will first look at a new model of leadership in Chapter 4.

## Summary

1.  When organizations are confronted with situations involving high levels of uncertainty, they need to question their vision of the future rigorously and continuously. Organizations that only plan for the "most probable" future will sooner or later be surprised by a different "unforeseen" future. This can be avoided by proactively taking a variety of possible futures into account. *Futures thinking* offers a method to accomplish this.

2.  *Futures thinking* requires new methods that will allow people *to learn* from the future. This should be linked to the existing methods and processes of decision-making, based on strategic management. This new process, together with the corresponding new leadership culture that makes this possible, is known as a *strategic conversation*.

3.  Strategic scenario planning and horizon scanning support strategic conversations. Both are monitored by a measuring system that makes possible the early detection of fundamental changes in the environment and develops hypotheses about the forces and drivers on which the future will unfold (*early warning systems*).

4.  A scenario plan is a chronological description or roadmap of a series of events. It is a coherent set of assumptions that forms the basis for future projections. A future projection is a description of a possible, probable or plausible future.

5.  Uncertainty is not the same as the absence of predictability: *futures thinking* is situated in the area where *uncertainty increases* and *predictability decreases*.

6.  A future project requires a good definition of its objectives. This will make possible the selection of an appropriate approach. Two questions can help:

    *   Is it a one-off project or is it an ongoing process as part of creating a learning organization?
    *   Is it a future exploration project or must it also allow decisions to be taken in the present?

7.  *Sensemaking* in respect of future environments offers little value unless action plans and basic strategies, which are *robust* against changing environments, are also developed.

8. Strategy and value creation in turbulent environments must be accompanied by thinking about the robustness of strategy. Thinking about models and predictions or about flexibility is equally important, but it remains subordinate, because it does not contribute towards the development of a learning organization.

# Chapter 4
# No future without leaders

*"Life can only be understood backwards; but it must be lived forwards."*
Søren A. Kierkegaard (1813-1855)

Sometimes we joke by saying that in today's world the only certain thing is un-certainty. The crisis faced by Sir David King (*cf.* prologue) may appear exceptional at first glance. The fundamental change in the business model of our pharma-ceutical company (*cf.* chapter 2) might also seem exceptional. Yet nothing could be further from the truth. Crises – which according to the statisticians only take place on average once every 70 years – now take place almost daily. Crises such as pandemics and financial crashes, or more profound transformations such as the industrialization of new growth countries. In short, change is here to stay. And it will increase each and every day.

In this chapter, we will study in detail an important aspect of this constant state of upheaval: the fact that all these changes arise, with no exceptions, in the envi-ronment of the organization. Other more sudden and more dramatic changes have their origin in a global environment that is increasingly showing a greater level of interdependency. Because of globalization, changes seem to happen as though they have been induced by a worldwide fabric of increasing connectedness. This interconnectedness manifests itself in new and often unexpected combina-tions of macro-environmental factors, summarized in the well-known anagrams PEST or STEEP and by their extensions PESTLED[41], SPECTRE and STEEPLED. The letters employed in these anagrams stand for **S**ociological, **T**echnological, **E**conomic, **E**cological & **E**nvironmental, **P**olitical, **L**egal, **E**thical, **D**emographical, **R**egulatory and **C**ultural. The use of such anagrams underlines the increasing importance of macro-environmental factors. Early strategy literature knew only of the PEST-analysis, but since then this has evolved into PESTLED and even this new anagram seems likely to have a few more new letters added before long!

While a single stand-alone organization is not really able to have any serious impact on these macro-environmental factors, the opposite is definitely not the case. Newly emerging changes most certainly have an impact on organizations and even on countries. Consequently, it is important to focus on the impact of context on organizations and to understand the implications, consequences and challenges this presents to leaders when dealing with such environments.

## Leadership follows environment

The financial, economic and subsequent political crisis of 2008, which is now often referred to as the 'Great Recession' – although perhaps a better name would be the 'Contained Depression' – has frequently been compared to another formidable crisis: the Great Depression of the 1930s. However, a more detailed examination reveals some major differences, explaining why the names have been chosen differently. The crisis of the 1930s took place within the existing economic production model, while the recent crisis not only lies on a fault line of transition from an industrial society to a knowledge-based society, but was also subject to an entirely different set of dynamics.

A purely Keynesian approach at the macroeconomic level will not suffice on this occasion, while at the micro-economic level many businesses, corporations and enterprises have learned by now that proven methods from the past will no longer suffice either. On the contrary, they will most likely make the situation worse.

The dynamics, uncertainty, complexity and turbulence at play within the current environment require a new form of leadership. This new type of leadership – imposed by the environment – must be able to anticipate and understand new and better adapted strategy methodologies based on future thinking, allowing modern leaders to interact with the equally new forms of networking, relationship and cooperation, as depicted in Figure 5.

To explain this in more detail, we will first elaborate on the characteristics of this new environment, before moving on to study the challenges of leadership and characteristics required of leaders to be effective in this new context.

**Figure 5: Model of new leadership**

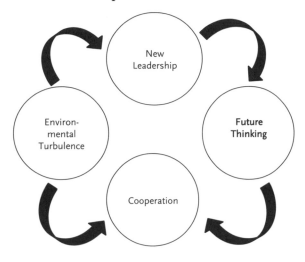

Model for New Leadership

## The new business environment: turbulence

What is the relationship between the characteristics of the business environment and the survival of an organization within that environment?

This subject – studied and known under its scientific name *congruence theory* – has been at the centre of organization and strategic management theory for more than 60 years. Congruence theory proposes that *the performance of an organization improves as the organization adjusts, fits or lines up (i.e. it is more congruent) to its external environment.*

*Strategy, structure* and internal *systems* and processes also all need to be constantly brought in line with the changing characteristics of the environment. It is like a skipper (internal) who trims his sail continuously to the wind (external) to reach his destination (*i.e. dynamic congruence*). This concept of congruence or *strategic fit* is recognized today as a central and fundamental paradigm of strategy, and is considered essential for the survival of any organization.[42]

Frederick (Fred) Edmund Emery (1925-1997) and Eric Trist (1909-1993) investigated this same matter in the 1960s, but looked at the subject from a completely different angle, since both were researchers in social psychology at the Tavistock

Institute in London. For their research, they were inspired by *open system thinking*, which K. Ludwig von Bertalanffy (1901-1972) had developed from biology and W. Ross Ashby (1903-1972) from the organization and control of complex systems and cybernetics.

Unlike an object, a biological organism has an 'open' relationship with the environment: it imports substances from the environment, which it transforms using its own system, and then exports other elements back to that environment (*cf.* metabolism). By this process, the organism gets the energy it needs to allow stability. Stability is needed to adapt to variety in the environment, which is necessary to survive and thrive.

Open system thinking developed into a domain that went far beyond biology. It also proved to be applicable to social phenomena. Emery and Trist were pioneers, who used *open systems thinking* in organizations that also have an 'open' relationship with their environment. The two researchers developed a classification, which they called the *causal texture* of that environment. In 1965, they published their conclusions in *Human Relations*.[43] This publication laid the foundations for more recent publications to build on their findings. Emery and Trist distinguished four causal ambient textures, one of which received more attention than the other three: they called this fourth environment *'turbulent'*, after they both experienced this phenomenon on an airplane. It is this turbulent ambient category in particular that demands our attention in a futures context.

## The theory of causal texture

The theory of causal texture is about systems that try to survive and thrive in their environment. The organization (system) and the environment evolve together, because they influence each other. Organization and environment do not simply have connections between internal variables, but also between each other.

Emery and Trist distinguished four[44] theoretical levels of environments in an order of increasing *complexity* and *connectedness*, and with an increasing degree of *structure in the interweaving* of the constituent parts: the causal texture.

*Complexity* reflects for Emery and Trist the richness of the surrounding elements, in particular the number of new or possible connections and the emergence of new interdependencies. The connectedness of the variables between the systems and the environment is a means to decode and analyse this complexity. The causal structure determines how and to what extent the environment will be organized or structured. In other words, the extent to which and the manner in which the variables and the relationships between them are causally connected or interwoven.

This relates to connections or links arising from a certain causal logic, which remains valid for a longer period of time. Emery and Trist called these connections *law-like connections*.

**Figure 6: Model of an open system**

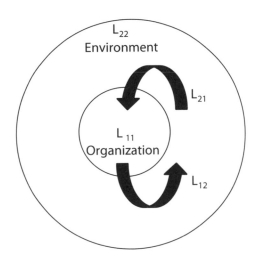

*Source*: based on Ramirez R., Oxford Scenarios Programme

The connections that are internal to the organization are identified with $L_I$ (L comes from *link* or *law-like connection* and the 'I' indicates that it concerns internal connections within the organization itself). The connections that exist in the environment are identified with $L_2$ (where '2' obviously refers to connections with the external environment).This means that there are four possible connections (Figure 6):

- $L_{II}$ (read as L one-one) indicates connections that remain internal to the organization. These are internal dependencies or interdependencies. For example, the processes in the organization itself.

- $L_{12}$ connects the system with the environment. Here we are talking about transactional interdependencies: the *outputs* of the organization. For example, the products or services they bring to market or the pollution they emit.
- $L_{21}$ connects the environment with the system. These are again transactional interdependencies; in particular, the inputs of the organization. For example, the products that are purchased from suppliers, or learning processes.
- $L_{22}$ connects elements in the environment, in the causal texture. These are the interdependencies that occur within the environment itself. For example, the combination of the interactions between scarcity of water, which makes agriculture difficult, causing food shortages, which leads to migration, causing political tension within the indigenous population, who feel threatened by the influx.

Depending on which connections or links ($L_{11}$, $L_{12}$, $L_{21}$ and $L_{22}$) are most important, there can be four theoretical environments or causal texture types.

## Type I: calm and random environment

In this first (theoretical) type, we find the means, the objectives and the good and bad elements (meaning the elements that have a good or bad influence on the behaviour of the organization) randomly distributed in the environment. This is similar to what economists call the *perfect market*. The organization that operates in such an environment does not need to distinguish between tactics and strategy. The optimal strategy is purely and simply the *tactic* to 'instinctively' do its best on a local basis. Think of the trader on a flea market:[45] the seller has no idea when his next customer will show up, but as soon as a potential buyer appears, he is only concerned with getting the most favourable deal for himself, devoting little further attention to subsequent customer satisfaction. In this kind of environment, tactics are sufficient.

## Type II: calm and clustered environment

Although this situation is slightly more complex, it is still a placid environment. Resources, goals and good and bad elements are no longer randomly scattered, but are in some way linked or clustered. In economic terms, this is an imperfect market with market failures. Survival in such an environment will be difficult, if the organization only reacts on a tactical level to every possible variation in the environment.

A new element therefore needs to be added to the organization's repertoire of responses: *strategy*, which is not the same as tactics. Survival increasingly depends on what the organization knows about its environment. Just aiming for an obvious goal can sometimes bring the organization into dangerous waters, while immediately bypassing difficulties can sometimes lead the organization away from a potentially rewarding position. In a clustered environment, it is therefore important that an optimal position is found, precisely because the environment is no longer randomly distributed and because some positions are more profitable than others. For this, the organization needs to concentrate its resources on a major plan (*i.e.* strategy) and develop distinctive competencies to reach the strategic goal. That is why a greater degree of centralization and control is required.

The choice of the strategy determines the level of possibility to adapt to the environment much more strongly than with the 'tactics' in type I. The more accurate and precise knowledge of the environment, the easier this task becomes.

## Type III: disturbed and reactive environment

In the first two types, a majority of actors will feel and assess the environment as stable. In type III, with ever more interconnections and hence a greater degree of complexity, this stability is more dynamic or 'disrupted'. But even if competition in this type is fierce and organizations sometimes vanish from the scene, it all happens reasonably legitimately. For this reason, the actors themselves may continue to recognize this type of environment as relatively stable. This is comparable with what economists call an oligopoly, a market with a limited number of dominant players. It is, in fact, a type II-environment, but with multiple players who are very similar. This is the dominant feature of the type III-environment.

In this environment, each organization must take into account the actions of other – similar – organizations. Each organization must also learn as much as it can about the environment. Other players aspire to the same position that your organization wants to make its own in the long term. Consequently, each player tries to increase its chances by disrupting everyone else's.

Strategy still involves to some extent the selection of a strategic goal – where does the organization want to end up in the future? – while tactics in this instance is a matter of selecting an immediate action from a range of available options. This creates an intermediate level of response: the *operational level*. A strong operational level is required to determine the sequence of actions that need to be taken, but also to define the actions required to weaken the competition or put them in an unfavourable position. The purpose of the operational level is actually to plan for a series of tactical initiatives and to estimate the likely reaction of the other players. In turn, these reactions will require further new responses. This process is comparable to what happens in a chess game or a war game or is explained by game theory.[46] In this continuous exchange of action and reaction, quality and speed of decision-making is of crucial importance. However, this requires flexibility, which means that decentralization is necessary.

This type of environment is less about capturing strategic positions or building distinctive capabilities to develop such strategic positions. In this environment, the mission is to survive the fierce competitive battles. Consequently, the strategies of absorption and parasitism are of paramount importance, applied through the tactics of mergers and acquisitions. A degree of stability can also be promoted through a certain level of understanding between similar players: every organization in this environment wants to avoid specific and deadly competitive battles in certain domains.

Table 3 presents a summary of the main characteristics of the four causal textures, allowing us to follow how the situation of the organization changes, depending on which connections or links $L_{nn}$ become prominent. However, we will first discuss the most relevant causal texture.

## Type IV: turbulent environment

The most complex environment in which it is still possible to adapt to changes is type IV: the turbulent environment. In types I to III, change occurs between organizations that are part of a relatively predictable environment: not always pleasant and certainly with its ups and downs, but still relatively stable. In type IV, however, the picture is very different, since the contextual environment ($L_{22}$-connections) is itself a source of instability.

**Table 3: The four causal textures**

| Type | Structure | Most prominent connections | Characteristics of success in this type |
|------|-----------|----------------------------|------------------------------------------|
| **I. Calm and random** | • Resources, goals and good and bad elements are randomly distributed in the field<br>• Conditions of the perfect market | $L_{11}$ | • Tactics on the basis of experience<br>• Local optimization here and now |
| **II. Calm and clustered** | • The distribution of resources, goals and good and bad elements gives rise to superior positions<br>• Conditions of the imperfect market with market failures | $L_{11}+L_{21}$ | • Determine a strategy to access a superior position.<br>• Develop distinctive competencies<br>• Centralisation of operations |
| **III. Disturbed and reactive** | • Similar organizations in fierce competition<br>• Oligopoly<br>• More $L_{21}$ and $L_{12}$ connections than in previous types | $L_{11}+L_{12}+L_{21}$ | • Strategy based on game theory<br>• Communicating with others to influence inputs<br>• Setting up operational campaigns<br>• Quick decisions<br>• Relationship with others in the same field |
| **IV. Turbulent** | • The entire common basis (environment) is in motion<br>• $L_{22}$ is uncertain and changeable and begins to lead a life of its own<br>• The distinction between $L_{12}$-$L_{21}$ and $L_{22}$ fades | $L_{11}+L_{21}+L_{12}+L_{22}$<br><br>The distinction between 1 and 2 is vague | • Organizations that work together, survive.<br>• Strategies of cooperation between unequal organizations in the field. |

*Source:* based on Ramirez R., Selsky J.W., van der Heijden K. (2008), p. 20.

The common environmental basis of all players is in motion. When the $L_{22}$-connections become prominent and start to lead a life of their own, the need for interdependence grows, ranging from purely economic connections in the environment to legislation, regulation, technology and other broad social phenomena. The growing importance of, for example, research and technology, provides a permanent source of change and instability.

For organizations, this means a huge increase of uncertainty in their (relevant) environment. The players feel that they are no longer able to rely on the environment as they once knew it. They notice that the uncertainty is more prominent, in a new and different way.

The leaders of the organization must introduce new methods to survive in this changed environment. In fact, leaders who do not recognise the new situation and continue to use the procedures they employed in a more stable past – such as reactive actions to damage competitors or a unilateral focus on cost reduction in response to a corporate crisis – simply make the situation worse. In this way, the organizations, on an aggregate level, add more turbulence to the contextual environment through their own actions. In short, they also produce uncertainties themselves.

Managers, policy-makers and researchers alike quickly adopted the term 'turbulence'. They recognized the type of wicked problems they actually met in their daily environments, which continued to change quickly and with increasing uncertainty and complexity. This recognition contributed to a large extent to the subsequent 'fame' of Emery and Trist's 1965 paper, which is still one of the most-cited papers in management literature today.

Another important contribution to the domain was the identification of the $L_{22}$-connections that make an environment evolve and transform. We will discuss some of these connections in Chapter 6.

Over the course of time, however, there was an increasing degree of abstruseness about the distinction between the impact of both the $L_{21}$ and the $L_{22}$ connections. It is clear that $L_{21}$ represents the connections from the environment that have an impact on the organization. But the $L_{22}$-connections between variables in the environment also have an impact on the organization. So what is the difference between their respective impacts? Is there, in fact, any difference?

This was subsequently clarified by making a distinction between the *transactional environment* and the *contextual environment*. Each organization has its own specific competitive and collaborative connections with others, which are defined by the $L_{21}$ and $L_{12}$-connections. This is the transactional environment, which is determined by the actions of the actors in the organizations. All these transactions together (*i.e.* aggregated) are part of the contextual environment. This contextual environment is determined by the relevant $L_{22}$-connections, expressed as factors on a macro level, not as the actions of agents. Figure 7 gives a visual representation of this.

The contextual environment consists of the big 'macro' phenomena, such as demographic evolution, geopolitical trends and the prices of energy and raw materials, as well as their relative degree of interconnectedness. The organization can neither control nor influence these factors, but can still investigate them and make estimates about their impact.

The transactional environment relates to the different external parties who enter into transactions with the organization; for example, customers, suppliers and investors. The organization can influence these relationships and to some extent can even shape them to serve its objectives.

Finally, the smallest circle in Figure 7 represents the organization, which has its operations fully under its own control.

**Figure 7: The transactional and the contextual environment**

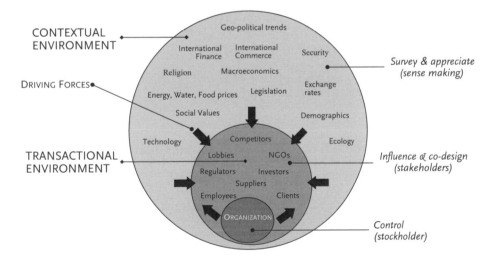

*Source:* adapted from Ramirez R., Oxford Scenarios Programme.

So what exactly defines the distinction between the transactional environment and the contextual environment? Well, if an individual actor or organization can influence the situation, we are talking about the transactional environment, defined by the $L_{12}$ and the $L_{21}$-connections. If an individual actor looks at macro phenomena that he or she cannot personally or directly influence, we are talking about the contextual environment, defined by the $L_{22}$-connections.

In the first three types of causal textures, actors preserve a certain degree of control over the situation on an aggregated level. However, in the turbulent causal texture the $L_{12}$ and $L_{21}$-connections are influenced by the highly uncertain $L_{22}$-macro relationships, which cannot be controlled but only examined and assessed. Because this source of uncertainty ($L_{22}$) is no longer predictable in turbulent causal textures, scenario thinking becomes very relevant. Consequently, it is essential that the methodology on which the strategic scenario thinking rests does not use probabilities or predictabilities to explore how turbulence will eventually manifest itself.

In the academic publications of Emery and Trist, the four types are clearly marked out. In practice, this distinction is sometimes much harder to make, because different actors have a different perception of the degree of turbulence. Some people will think that they are operating in a truly turbulent texture, while others will position themselves in a more disruptive-reactive texture. This difference in interpretation of the environment is related to a difference in the perception of their own capacity for adjustment: for example, some believe they can better adapt to the environment by committing more and more resources, while others do not see how this will make any difference.

## Why does a turbulent or VUCAT environment disturb?

The ever-increasing interdependencies between contextual variables and factors ($L_{22}$) ensure that twists, turns and unexpected events with a great impact on the organization will occur more regularly. Before 2008, it was difficult to explain this phenomenon to decision-makers in the bank and insurance industry. Managers from the energy and telecommunications sectors understood this much better: they had experienced turbulence as a result of the different oil shocks or when the internet bubble burst in 2001. The bankers and insurers finally began to get the message after the start of the 2008 financial crisis – even if by 2016 some seem to have forgotten most of it again.

What does this show? It suggests that we first have to experience turbulence in order to understand what it means. But after the storm has passed and once the sun is shining again, we seem all too ready to go back to the old methods of 'business as usual'. Even responsible executives, ministers and chiefs of staff who question everything and lie awake at night when the survival of their organization is threatened by a sudden and unexpected shock in the environment rarely see that this turbulence is becoming an increasingly common reality.

We have named this new reality a *VUCAT environment* (Volatility, Uncertainty, Complexity, Ambiguity and Turbulent). The acronym VUCA was first used in the 1990s by the U.S. War College to describe the capability to engage with environments marked by rapid change and complexity, which inevitably pose huge planning challenges. This requires increased attention for strategic decision-making, readiness planning, risk management, problem-solving, future thinking and sensemaking. VUCA has since been borrowed by business leaders to describe a complex and chaotic world. However, the challenge of leadership in a VUCAT world demands a new way of thinking and a whole new set of skills. VUCAT environments have risen to the top of the management agenda in recent years, because the incidence of shocks and surprises is now so frequent that leaders can no longer avoid them! NIMTO (Not In My Term of Office) has seen dropping the 'Not' to become IMTO. As a result, leaders are increasingly forced to come up with solutions to *unpredictable* and *high impact* challenges from within their environment, which explains their increasing interest in complexity theory, foresight and future thinking.

## Why is turbulence so problematic?

The characteristics of a turbulent causal texture are consecutive changes, high uncertainty and complexity. Various academic disciplines have indicated the uncomfortable consequences of uncertainty: (a) psychologists draw attention to the harmful effects of stress and adversity (*e.g.* in times of war, during the restructuring of companies, *etc.*) and emphasize that uncertainty undermines the sense of identity of individuals; (b) anthropologists and sociologists point out that the dismantling or downsizing of structures is a bad solution for dealing with uncertainty and often leads to passivity and/or conflicts; (c) political scientists examine why conflicts are caused by uncertainty over the availability of critical resources (*e.g.* oil, water, food, *etc.*); (d) economists explain how uncertainty or lack of predictability destroys opportunities for long-term investments (*e.g.* who wants to risk investing in an expensive hydroelectric power plant if there is uncertainty about future water flows, because the snow on the mountains that feeds rivers and eventually the dam is melting as a result of global warming?). Everything starts with the recognition of a turbulent environment.

## How to survive in a turbulent environment

What can you do if your organization ends up in a turbulent causal texture? How can you escape its negative and harmful effects?

The most important thing to remember is that an organization will never be able to adjust to this new and harsh environment on its own. Stability cannot be achieved through individual action; nor can it be achieved through clever tactics and/or strategy (which is the case in disturbed and reactive environments). In short, the individual organization cannot escape the harmful effects of a turbulent environment using direct action.

In type IV environments, organizations need to work together with other organizations that are different but whose fate is positively correlated (*cf.* networking to reduce uncertainty). In these turbulent type IV environments, it is necessary for organizations to find or to create areas of cooperation, so that they can act together. This is much less the case in type III environments. In these environments, competition is fierce, because the fate of similar organizations is negatively correlated. Or to put it differently: in turbulent environments organizations need to define common values that they can institutionalize and that will enable them to create a mutual basis for collaboration.

A practical application of this can be observed, for example, when organizations embrace the concept of 'open innovation'.[47] This might involve a (large) company cooperating in a two-way process with other organizations, such as research institutes, start-ups, spin-offs from university research, *etc.*, to realize innovations. Sadly, however, this kind of co-operation is all too often lacking. Looking in retrospect at the disaster on the *Deepwater Horizon* drilling platform in the Gulf of Mexico in 2010, one wonders how it is possible that the major oil companies had not previously cooperated to prepare for the challenge of a possible (plausible) accident of this kind. The failure to recognize a turbulent environment can sometimes be very costly. Just ask BP!

Turbulent environments therefore mean that organizations will have to rely more and more on outsiders, on 'others'. This can only happen if common values exist between these outsiders and the organization. Professional industry associations already have experience in this field and can provide possible models. The aim is to create islands in which organizations can work together, thereby blocking or reducing turbulence.

In this volatile environment, strategic goals can no longer be formulated in simple terms, such as a superior position (type II) or operational tactics and distinctive abilities (type III). In these new circumstances, goals and objectives must be expressed in terms of *institutionalization*. Organizations are becoming institutions through the assimilation and incorporation of broader social values that connect them more closely to the social environment. Put simply, the CEO becomes a statesman, but without much formal training, education or preparation and without any democratic legitimization or control. This explains perhaps the increasing importance of *corporate social responsibility* (CSR) in recent years.

This institutionalization becomes a source of stability, providing the objectives of one organization take account of the interests of the other parties involved. However, the great enemy to the acceptance of these new values is time. The literature speaks in terms of years (generations) when discussing changing attitudes and the acceptance of new values. But time is often the commodity least available in turbulent situations.

In turbulent environments, it is necessary to shift the focus from the competitive struggle within the existing transactional environment – with increasingly stronger competition as the turbulence increases – to a better understanding of how the forces of the contextual environment ($L_{22}$) can shape the transactional environment.

It is precisely this new focus that constitutes the essence of future thinking: working through a set of possible scenarios in the contextual environment and examining the consequences of these scenarios on the transactional environment and on the organization.

## The relationship between future thinking and context

Before setting up cooperation between organizations, it is imperative to estimate first the nature of the turbulent causal texture. What kind of new behaviour does this new environment require? By exploring a set of different scenarios and not just a single ideal scenario (because this would be a prediction), managers and policy-makers will see and understand more easily that the contextual environment is beyond their area of influence and control. This realization – that they cannot influence the environment directly – is essential as a preparation for a cooperative process that will exclude turbulence for all its participants.

This is easily said, but in practice it can sometimes be quite a problem. Creating and institutionalizing new rules and regulations also means a return to an increase in the competitive intensity that characterizes the type III 'disturbed and reactive' causal texture. Creating turbulence-free areas can only be successful when there is enough freedom to discuss and debate different perspectives, and when each perspective is taken seriously and is regarded as useful and legitimate. Future thinking stimulates this process through *strategic conversations*. If these discussions and debates make it possible for cooperation to gain the upper hand over competitive self-interest, the scenarios can become effective. If however, competition wins from cooperation, the future thinking will fail. This happened in 2008, when banks were 'suddenly' no longer willing to lend via the interbank market to other banks, unless at an extortionate rate of interest.

In essence, the only way to stop the snowball-effect that turbulence causes, nourishes and is fed by, is to reduce the importance of the $L_{22}$-connections in the contextual environment by institutionalizing new values. The basic idea is that shared values can create an environment that is less uncertain than the causal texture of type IV environments, because turbulence is reduced and, consequently, a more stable basis for decision making and investing in the future is created.

At crucial decision-making moments in this process, there is a vital role for creative and innovative individuals who can see new ways to circumvent the confusion of the *wicked problems* that are caused by turbulence. Strategic scenario thinking as a new management method is a key element in this creative and imaginative process: it creates clarity in an unclear situation.

## Leadership in turbulent environments

The Saïd Business School, University of Oxford, published in 2015 one of the most comprehensive in-depth studies[48] on the challenges faced by global leaders managing in turbulent environments. The central research question was this: "What are the critical capabilities senior leaders need to succeed in an environment marked by uncertainty, complexity and constant change?"

The research findings indicated that leaders managing change in turbulent global environments mainly put the emphasis on speed of reaction. However, a preoccupation with this single dimension may misdirect management attention towards events that seem urgent, but are, in fact, of limited scope or significance. To manage effectively, leaders need not only to focus on speed but must pay equal attention to the *speed, scope* and *significance* ($S^3$) of each challenge they face – or so the research suggests. The second dimension – *the scope of the change* – relates to the extent to which a particular event or trend is far-reaching. The greater the scope of change, the more likely it will become significant and affect the organization. The third dimension – *the significance of the change* – refers to how deeply any change impacts on the organization.

Thoughtfully assessing the speed, scope and significance of change is essential in order to identify the decisions to delegate, determine the decisions to make, and dedicate sufficient time to think. Proper delegation gives leaders more time to pace the decisions they have to make and creates space for constructive open debate or strategic conversations. This is not a process that needs to be limited to the executive team, but can also involve members of the board and external experts.

Predicting and re-assessing the significance of all three dimensions as the data continues to accumulate is crucial. It means asking "how, how fast and how much" an event will impact on the organization. Furthermore, in order to anticipating how, when and why the different contexts may interact to cause disruption, an organization needs to develop an early warning system (EWS), geared to the personal use of the leader and conceptualized as *ripple intelligence*. Ripple intelligence, according to Michael Smets (CEO Report, 2015), enables leaders to envision how trends and contexts may intersect and change direction, so that they can anticipate disruptions, make time to plan, and protect against being blindsided by unexpected events. But ripple intelligence also makes leaders aware of their own impact and how it may influence contexts that might otherwise seem remote and unconnected. As already indicated, one of the major advantages of future thinking is its ability to visualize the interactions of simultaneous events "as ripples on a pond". This can help leaders to expect the unexpected and thus be more prepared to seize opportunities or avoid or contain wicked problems.

Ripple intelligence becomes even more effective as leaders learn to harness the "power of doubt". Leaders who accept doubt – defined as a positive state that is both emotional and intellectual – can select different strategies to mobilize their doubts in the service of better decisions. Such skills are crucial in an environment where chasing certainty is often futile.

Acknowledging doubt as both a feeling and as an information issue helps to distinguish constructive doubt from disruptive second-guessing. From a 'thinking futures' perspective, the taking of decisions with limited information is of particular interest. Leaders who are comfortable making decisions with limited information often rely on their experience or intuition. However, the need to operate in highly complex and uncertain environments often makes experience and intuition irrelevant. Figure 8 shows the four different situations that can confront a leader when dealing with strategic decision-making in turbulent situations.

Although all four situations can and regularly do occur, experience suggests that in reality it is very difficult as a leader to know in which situation you actually find yourself, since it all depends on how you assesses your own level of knowledge.

The two most preferable situations to promote 'thinking futures' are those when leaders realize they have insufficient or limited knowledge about a situation: (1) *Low Knowledge/No Fear* LK/NF or (2) *Low Knowledge/High Anxiety* LK/HA (*cf.* Figure 8). A realization that they lack knowledge compels the leader to be open to listening, willing to ask questions and available to listen to alternatives. Consequently, if organizations want to remedy 'low knowledge' situations, creating an appropriate learning culture will be a critical key success factor: either to fully understand and apply the methods of futures thinking or to build a learning organization (*cf.* strategic conversations, continuing learning).

**Figure 8: The feeling – knowing leadership nexus**

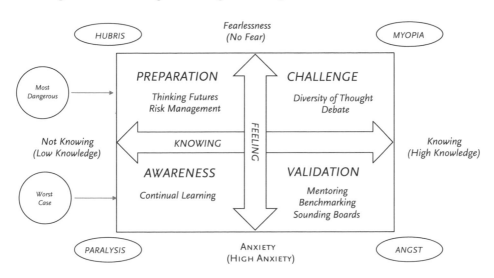

*Source*: adapted from Saïd Business School, *CEO Report* (2015).

In both 'low knowledge' situations, the leader must stimulate constructive conflict, by using an angle of vision not yet seen by others. These angles strengthen the leader's ripple intelligence. Even so, achieving success with 'constructive challenge' debates or strategic conversations at executive level is difficult and requires the leader to expressly invite dissenting visions or else risk finding false validation for his own ideas, which reinforce the very myopia he seeks to mitigate.

Both situations involve clear risks. The confident leader 'who knows best' but actually has low knowledge (LK/NF) runs the risk of 'hubris'. This can be avoided by careful preparation, using such methods as scenario planning, worst-case scenarios, long-term planning, contingency planning, *etc*. In other words, by thinking futures! The non-confident leader who realizes his lack of knowledge (LK/HA) presents a different risk: 'paralysis'. The remedy here is continual learning, which includes wide and deep reading, data collection, expert advice and conversations with a wide variety of people.

*New leadership for turbulent environments requires that:*

- Focus is placed on asking the right questions;
- Strategic teams are actively open to the input of external experts and to new developments in their environment;
- Effort is made to promote cooperation and working together;
- Sufficient data is collected and multiple interpretations are elaborated about the future evolutions of the environment;
- The discussion of these interpretations becomes a regular, systematic and continuous process and is not considered a one-off effort;
- The leader takes on the role of coach and facilitator, which contributes to the process of regular and documented strategic conversations;
- The leader ensures that team members understand and take up their responsibilities;
- Sufficient time is taken to formulate better and more appropriate answers;
- All these efforts must be sustained.

*What happened to our pharmaceutical company after the working group reported to the board of directors? A shock went through the entire organization. The working group's scenario exercise brought a disruptive clarity in the definition of the problem. The conclusion was that the business model that had been so successful in the past was no longer valid. The cost of research and the reduced guarantee of new discoveries necessitated a very different model for the future. The expectation that increasing pressure on public budgets would reduce the refund capacities of health insurance schemes also caused uncertainty, particularly in view of the increased ageing of the population. So what did they need to do?*

*To cut a long story short: the increasingly turbulent environment means that the time has come for our pharmaceutical company to switch to a different business model. A model based on broader and more intense cooperation, affecting not only the company, but also the entire business eco-system, including the pharmaceutical industry as a whole. In this way, the company can focus on prevention rather than on curative medicine that requires unaffordable research and will no longer be supported in future by dwindling public expenditure. In order to eliminate turbulence, cooperation with different partners in the eco-system will be necessary: from the health service and biotech companies to ICT and food companies, with whom new revenue models can be built on data driven models that allow for individualised treatments, multidisciplinary approaches and preventive healthcare programmes, for example, to create preventive testing over the internet or to develop safe nutrition with health-giving effects (e.g. low cholesterol drinks). The essential precondition for such cooperation is the definition of common values accepted by all parties concerned.*

## Summary

1. In a turbulent environment, a new form of leadership is needed that incorporates future thinking and promotes cooperation.

2. The main characteristic of this new leadership is that the leader must organize *strategic conversations* by focusing debates of the future and, in particular, on the future environment. This process is based on future thinking. The leader must also make a substantive contribution of his own.

3. Fred Emery and Eric Trist studied the relationship between an organization and its surroundings. They distinguished four types of causal textures and in each type different interdependencies are dominant. The most relevant type is the *turbulent texture*, in which a fabric of interdependencies between variables in the environment provides great uncertainty and results in turbulence for organizations that operate in this environment.

4. Managers and politicians experience this turbulence and recognize it in the form of *wicked problems*. To escape the negative consequences of a turbulent environment, cooperation with other organizations with a positive correlation will be necessary. In addition, new values will need to be institutionalized.

# Chapter 5
# From thinking to doing

*"The illiterate of the future will not be the person who cannot read.*
*It will be the person who does not know how to learn."*
Alvin Toffler (°1928)

In the previous chapter, we proposed a new model for leadership to survive in a turbulent environment. Strategic scenario-based thinking is an important part of that model. This method allows a flexible and learning organization to be created. But how does such a scenario process actually work in practice? How do you implement this in an organization? These are the questions we will look at in this chapter. But first we will examine the differences between the classical methods and the scenario method. We will follow this up by describing the method as a roadmap applied to a simple example: the testing of a business strategy. Finally, we will illustrate a further application of the method, this time in relation to a conflict situation at an important moment in the recent history of South Africa.

## Selecting the most appropriate method

Over recent decades, many research methods based on scientific principles have been developed to master, understand or predict future developments. Rafael Popper (2008b) compiled an interesting taxonomy of some of the most frequently used methodologies and techniques for strategic foresight or futures research. Popper is a research fellow at the *Manchester Institute of Innovation Research* (MIoIR) at the University of Manchester and a member of the *European Foresight*

*Platform* (EFP).[49] In order to classify the different methods, he asked himself how teams would select the futures method they wanted to use. This question is more interesting than one might think. In practice, teams do not select a futures method on the sole basis of their preference for a qualitative or quantitative method; the selection is also influenced by the available competencies within the team to process and collect information.

**Figure 9: Taxonomy of futures research methodologies**

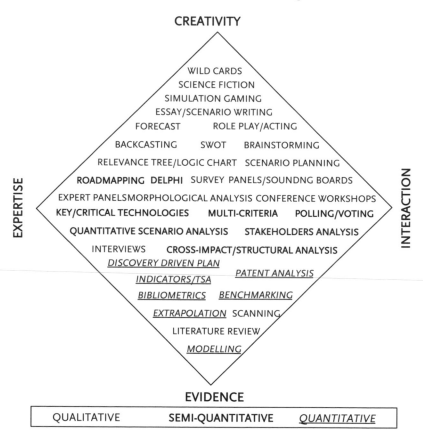

CREATIVITY

WILD CARDS
SCIENCE FICTION
SIMULATION GAMING
ESSAY/SCENARIO WRITING
FORECAST          ROLE PLAY/ACTING
BACKCASTING     SWOT    BRAINSTORMING
RELEVANCE TREE/LOGIC CHART  SCENARIO PLANNING
ROADMAPPING  DELPHI  SURVEY  PANELS/SOUNDNG BOARDS
EXPERT PANELSMORPHOLOGICAL ANALYSIS  CONFERENCE WORKSHOPS
KEY/CRITICAL TECHNOLOGIES      MULTI-CRITERIA      POLLING/VOTING
QUANTITATIVE SCENARIO ANALYSIS      STAKEHOLDERS ANALYSIS
INTERVIEWS    CROSS-IMPACT/STRUCTURAL ANALYSIS
*DISCOVERY DRIVEN PLAN*
*PATENT ANALYSIS*
*INDICATORS/TSA*
*BIBLIOMETRICS  BENCHMARKING*
*EXTRAPOLATION* SCANNING
LITERATURE REVIEW
*MODELLING*

EXPERTISE

INTERACTION

EVIDENCE

| QUALITATIVE | SEMI-QUANTITATIVE | *QUANTITATIVE* |
|---|---|---|

*Source*: adapted from Popper (2008b).

Based on a review and an analysis of numerous foresight studies, Popper concluded that four selection criteria could explain the preferences of a team for a specific futures research methodology. These four criteria are *creativity*, *evidence*, *expertise* and *interaction*. For example, a team that has resourcefulness and creativity as its major team assets will choose a creative method. In contrast, an interactive method will appeal more to teams wishing to emphasis the value of a shared vision among experts and non-experts. A team with a propensity for evidence based statements will select a method grounded in evidenced-based data, indicators and indices. Finally, an expert-driven methodology is likely to be chosen by teams composed of experts in their own right: people who combine extensive knowledge with years of experience, often with privileged access to relevant information or to a network with a huge amount of experience and exceptional, often non-tacit, know-how (*cf. Remarkable People*). Figure 9 provides an overview of the different methods according to Popper's classification.

Table 4 presents an additional overview of the characteristics of the different futures research methods.[50] A dark grey box indicates the dominant primary characteristic of a method, while a light grey box indicates secondary or additional characteristics. The table shows that the different futures methods can be grouped by *qualitative, quantitative, explorative, predictive* (*i.e.* a belief that there is one 'most likely' future) or *normative* (*i.e.* a belief in a future 'as it should be') properties. It also shows different ways in which these different methods create clarification and insight:

- Diagnosis: to understand what happens;
- Prognosis: to understand what might happen;
- Prescription: to define what must be done.

## Table 4: Characteristics of futures research methods

| Futures Thinking Methods | Diagnose | Prognoses | Prescriptive | Normative | Qualitative | Quantitative | Explorative | Predictive |
|---|---|---|---|---|---|---|---|---|
| Agent Modelling (*e.g.* MACTOR) | ■ | | | | | ▦ | | ▦ |
| SWOT-Analysis | ■ | | | | ▦ | | | |
| Environmental Scanning & Monitoring/EWS | ■ | | | | ▦ | | | |
| System Dynamics | ■ | | | | | ▦ | | ▦ |
| Structural Analyse (*e.g.* MICMAC) | ■ | | | | ▦ | | | ▦ |
| Discovery Driven Planning | ■ | ▦ | | | ▦ | | | ▦ |
| Creativity Methods (Brainstorming, Mind Mapping...) | ▦ | ■ | | ▦ | | | ▦ | |
| Expert Panels | | ■ | | ▦ | ▦ | | ▦ | |
| Relevance Tree/Logic Charts | | ■ | | ▦ | ▦ | | ▦ | |
| Strategic Scenarios | | ■ | | | ▦ | | ▦ | |
| Trend & Extrapolation | ▦ | ■ | | | | ▦ | | ▦ |
| Modelling & Simulation | ▦ | ■ | | | | ▦ | | ▦ |
| Role Play/Gaming | | ■ | | | ▦ | | ▦ | |
| Cross-Impact Analyses (*e.g.* SMIC)/Structural Analysis | | ■ | | | ▦ | ▦ | | |
| Backcasting | | ▦ | ■ | | ▦ | | | ▦ |
| Critical Key Technology Analysis | | ▦ | ■ | | ▦ | | | ▦ |
| Multi-Criteria Analyse (*e.g.* MULITIPOL) | | | ■ | | ▦ | | | ▦ |
| Technical Roadmapping | | ▦ | | ■ | | | ▦ | ▦ |
| Delphi | ▦ | ▦ | ▦ | | ▦ | | ■ | |

■ Primary characteristics     ▦ Secondary characteristics

*Source*: based on Glenn & Gordon (2011).

Selecting a methodology implies that that the characteristics of the methodology must be taken into consideration. In practice, this means that selecting a well-fitted methodology for futures research remains a difficult exercise and relies on a degree of experience to find a good balance between the available methods. Short-sighted rules of thumb like "quantitative methods are superior to qualitative methods" are never a sign of wisdom. Such rules fail to recognize the complexity of the futures research. Albert Einstein summarized this idea beautifully when he said:

> *"Many of the things you can count, don't count.*
> *Many of the things you can't count, really count."*

The choice of a foresight method is primarily *dictated* by the nature of the problem (Figure 9) and only secondarily by the desired level of confidence. The culture of stakeholders and the team also plays a role: French companies often prefer a quantitative approach, while qualitative methods are generally preferred in the U.K. Experience shows that in handling complex problems both qualitative and quantitative methods have their advantages, disadvantages and utility. A good combination of both is usually a wise choice. For example, as a first step, a qualitative exploratory approach may be used to identify and clarify the underlying assumptions, before subsequently using quantitative modelling for simulations that allow a proper assessment and estimation of the limitations of the model to be made.

In this book, we have selected one of the most advanced methods for strategic foresight or futures research: *strategic scenario thinking*. Futures research based on strategic scenario thinking relies on all four criteria of the Popper classification (Figure 9). It combines collecting reliable data and information (*evidence*) with the creative processes of trying to imagine plausible futures (*creativity*). Experts are included in the process as well (*expertise*), in order to leverage their special knowledge and insights (*experience*). Finally, managing an organization requires the ability to reach a consensus based on a shared vision, which is realized through interactive methods (*interaction*). Moreover, strategic scenario thinking starts without any preference for a qualitative or quantitative method, since both are used. However, in our interpretation of the method we do follow a strict preference for the sequence in which these qualitative and quantitative methods are used. In order to understand what is happening and the issues at stake (*diagnosis*), the full richness of all the possibilities and options are first mapped using qualitative methods. Afterwards, and now with a much better understanding, we study what might possibly happen in the future (*i.e.* forecast). The accuracy of the quantitative evidence will deliver further support for the forecasts, with or without further use of methods that describe what should or should not happen (*cf.* prescriptive, normative or predicative).

## Urgently requested: better methods

The most commonly used method to understand what might happen in the future is the study of the past. In this way, we hope to predict the future. The most frequently used methods for forecasting, estimating or predicting are nearly all based on this principle of extrapolation: calculating future revenues; estimating the evolution of commodity prices; preparing budgets; estimating next year's GDP; estimating economic growth rates. All the macroeconomic and socio-demographic data used for the national budgeting process take historical data collection as their starting-point. Whichever way you look at it, it is difficult to avoid the conclusion that by using these methods the future is assumed to be fundamentally nothing more than a continuation of the past. At most, there are some minor adjustments: a slightly more optimistic or pessimistic prediction, or something of that nature. Yet for governments, enterprises, companies and many international organizations, these extrapolations are often the basis for multi-million dollar investment decisions and for important future strategy and policy options.

Taking strategic decisions always involves the future. And as we all know (or should know), you cannot predict the future by extrapolating the past – otherwise we would all be millionaires by now! In other words, the extrapolation method has some serious limitations.

The problem, however, lies mainly in the limitations of our own cognitive ability to learn. This is because our view of all possible alternatives or options for the future is limited by what we know from the past. This is a major problem in a world increasingly characterized by discontinuities, rapid change, growing complexity and uncertainty.

It is even worse when these so-called 'forecasts' receive official sanction from the company's senior management. By approving and explicitly communicating budgets and figures in this way, managers are effectively discouraging other people within the organization from trying to identify emerging forces, never mind actively detecting discontinuities that fall outside scope of this 'official future'. The bosses have already dictated how things are going to be – so why should anyone waste further energy on the matter? The result is that the organization is repeatedly surprised by discontinuous events. This increases the likelihood that major strategic opportunities will be missed. New strategic moves are especially important in times of discontinuity: just think of how the French bank BNP Paribas took the bold step of acquiring Fortis (one of the top European-ranked Belgian banks) in the middle of the 2008 financial crisis or how the Suez Group eventually gained control over the Société générale de Belgique holding company after the crisis created by the takeover raid of Carlo De Benedetti in 1988. Important strategic opportunities always arise when there are discontinuities. At such moments, strategy can really make the difference for those who are able to recognize the discontinuities in good time and are prepared to (re)act accordingly.

Another disadvantage of a single 'official future' is that debates about the future within these organizations tend to hide the risks instead of actively bringing them to light. The assumptions and prejudices on which the models, projections, forecasts and even the figures were built are quickly forgotten. This is disastrous in a world that is rapidly changing. It imposes a number of restrictions with important implications for strategy and policy. In particular, it restricts 'learning' from the bottom to the top of the organization. We all know organizations of this kind, which respond with painfully slowness to changes in the environment. *Futures thinking* circumvents these restrictions. The scenario method shifts the focus of leadership from a preoccupation with internal matters to the external environment, where most of the changes in the future will occur!

Moreover, *futures thinking* teaches people to think further than the implicit assumptions tacitly imposed by the past and to move beyond the restrictions sanctioned by the 'official future'. But to be effective, scenarios must also influence the mental images of the decision-makers about existing realities. If it fails to do this, the cause is lost.

In addition, the scenario method, based on the principles of *systems thinking*, has another significant advantage in comparison with the more commonly used methods of extrapolation: extrapolations limit themselves to rigorous projections relating to certain specific elements and figures; the scenario method essentially looks at the overall picture, at combinations and global interdependencies. It also aims to understand and interpret systems, not simply take snapshots of isolated elements.

Will real estate prices in some states of the U.S. rise or fall? A projection, no matter how sophisticated the model, will bring little understanding if that model does not take account of the system of sub-prime loans to customers who are barely solvent, the resale of these loans in repackaged debt claims, the global interdependence of banks and the out-of-control dependence on the major players in the interbank markets. Beautiful models often conceal these risks rather than bringing them to the surface. In complex systems, systems thinking can offer deeper insights by looking at the global picture, instead of an isolated and extremely precise projection of one particular aspect.

In Figure 10, we make an analogy with an iceberg. We see the world as we know it from television, from the *talking heads* or the *ticker tape* of the stock market and from the newspapers. But we pay hardly any attention to the underlying systems and interdependencies that have led to certain events. In these circumstances, there is a danger that we will only respond to events in a *defensive* or *reactive* way. Just as we do, for example, if we only see extrapolated turnover figures or the macro-projections that economists from economic and policy analysis departments continue to deliver to governments. As long as we prevent ourselves from trying to understand events as a system, we will not be able to work *proactively.* Instead, we will always be reactive – and therefore too late to react with impact.

**Figure 10: Systems thinking – the analogy with the iceberg**

News and Events

Patterns of System
Behaviour
(Trends)

System Structure
Causal relations
(Driving Forces)

*Source:* based on Senge P. (1990).

It is only when we dig deeper, without limiting ourselves by what we know from the past; it is only when we look at the big picture painted by systems, relationships and interdependencies; it is only then that we will learn more and obtain better insights about the future. It is only then that we will start to recognize *patterns* and will be able to identify significant *trends*. But the key to truly understanding the future lies hidden even deeper beneath the surface: it lies in understanding the *system structure*, in understanding the *causality* of the *relationships* and in understanding their interaction and effects. This requires attention to the interpretation process, which we call *sensemaking*. It is the only meaningful way to look at a possible impact of the future. It is the only way we can work proactively, allowing us to form opinions and develop options for discontinuous events. The scenario-based method creates a forum in which decision-makers can explore and test the impact of different (driving) forces and their combined effects.

The Swedish professor David Henschen Ingvar (1924-2000) conducted some particularly interesting research on this topic. He found that our human brain deals more effectively with the future if it can consider multiple alternatives. This is because we not only consider the alternatives but also memorize them afterwards: we therefore have *Memories of the Future*, as Ingvar formulated it. He concluded that we do this in order to filter environmental signals more quickly (*cf.* sense-making). All the information we pick up from the environment and which does not fit in with our memory of the future, we find unimportant. This allows us to make decisions between two and three times faster in times of crisis. He therefore proposed:

> *"We perceive something as meaningful if it fits with a memory we have made of an anticipated future."*

This means that people (and, according to Ingvar, probably organizations as well) who only have one future in mind see or hear very little. A company with one strategic plan or one fixed budget is virtually deaf and blind to change. In this respect, scenario-based thinking might be considered as the 'memory of the future' for an organization.

For example, when we prepare budgets, we are actually forming future expectations. Our budgets insert expectations about the future in our memory. In turbulent and rapidly changing environments, however, this encourages blindness towards shocks and changes. Our 'memory of the future' ensures that we no longer see things as they are. Our field of vision is smaller. So why do most companies still cherish their annual budgeting exercise?

Fortunately, it can be different – and better. Take Unilever, for example. This food giant has stopped their traditional annual budgeting, as was reported by *Controllers Magazine* on 21 May 2010. Unilever has replaced the annual budget with quarterly updated scenarios. According to financial controller Wim van der Windt, not only has forecast accuracy increased, but the company has become more entrepreneurial and more proactive as well. He claims that Unilever has swapped fixations for flexibility, replacing the static annual budgeting exercise with an ongoing activity that shifts the focus from internal negotiations to performance relative to the external competition. According to Unilever itself, this is:

*"No more than a necessary and logical adjustment to the current business requirements, because changes, unlike a few years ago, are not gradual anymore but come in shocks and are discontinuous."*

Markets are no longer local, but global. The limits of your capabilities are no longer defined by your amount of capital, but by your ideas. Consumers now have more power. Food companies like Unilever are therefore forced to be much more flexible – and static budgeting is not part of that new reality.

The power of the *memory of the future* can also be seen, by way of example, from the fact that many old maps continued to depict *California* as an island (Figure 11), even though an expedition in 1539 had proved that this was not the case. In 1496, the novel *Las Sergas de Esplandián*[51] by Garcia Rodriguez de Montalvo (1450-1504) was published, in which *California* was portrayed as a paradisiacal *island*,[52] populated entirely by women and ruled by Queen *Calafia*. It made no difference that expeditions reported that California was, in fact, a peninsula and not an island. The memory of the cartographers continued for a time to prevent a correct interpretation. It was only when people started to die in the desert carrying boats on their backs in the course of their desperate search to discover the 'riches' of the 'island' of California that King Ferdinand VI of Spain (1713-1759), known as *El Prudente*, finally decided that enough was enough. In 1747, he issued a Royal Order proclaiming once and for all that California was not an island. From then on, there were heavy penalties for making maps that depicted it as such. It is one of the greatest errors in the history of cartography, but by no means the only one. Maps of the 16th, 17th and even early 18th century show plenty of other non-existent islands in different parts of the world.

**Figure 11: Map of California anno 1639**

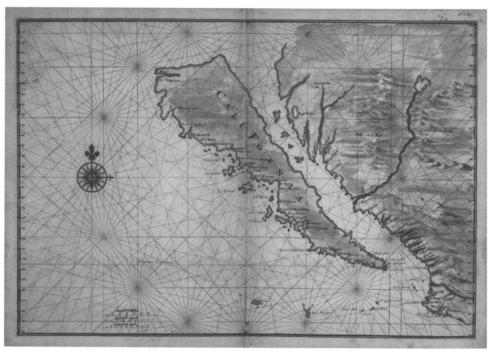

*Source: Johannes Vingboons, Amsterdam 1639 –* © American Library of Congress.

In his book *Obliquity*, John Kay points out that many of today's economists are still making predictions from a single dominant idea that denies reality. How many crises will be necessary before we understand that this methodology is deficient in our current, turbulent and fast changing environment? Recent economic models that failed to detect economic bubbles, banking crises, the debt crisis and the euro crisis can all be questioned (as can their authors) from a strictly scientific point of view about the validity of their knowledge. In fact, it is not unreasonable to ask whether a theory without predictive power can still be considered a theory.[53] According to Gregory Clark (2007, p. 371),[54] professor of economic history at the University of California at Davis, the failure of economic theory to predict and describe reality actually began as long ago as 1800! While the Malthusian model worked perfectly to understand, explain and predict the period prior to the industrial revolution, since then predictions based on economic models have demonstrated a continuous and steady decline in their ability to correctly predict the main macroeconomic parameters – although it is understandable that this proposition is not shared by everybody!

John Kay is not the only person to question the validity of current economic theory. The Hungarian-American businessman and philanthropist George Soros is also hugely frustrated by existing economic theories and models, but even more so by the fact that these models continue to be used by governments and central banks, notwithstanding their proven failure and limitations. Consequently, in 2012 he decided to endow the Oxford Martin School with 100 million dollars for fundamental and multi-disciplinary research in order to develop a new economic theory in cooperation with his think-tank, the *Institute for New Economic Thinking* (INET).

## Future thinking: a scenario roadmap in ten steps

*How does a strategic scenario exercise work in practice?*

All scenario exercises have a number of common elements: a relevant team is, of course, composed in advance and the purpose of the exercise is determined very precisely. The various steps are shown in Figure 12.

The *first step* is qualitative research. In a series of interviews we ask experts about their vision of the future. Later, this information is supplemented by *desk research* and quantitative data. It is important in this first step that we use a qualitative interview method, to explore the full richness of the different ideas.

The *second step* is the identification of key elements that may affect the problem. We find these key elements by analysing the interviews.

The *third step* starts with a group debate – a joint effort to collect different perspectives and visions. During this third step, the long list of key elements and uncertainties is reduced to a short list. Eventually, we select – again following a group debate – just two key elements for which the level of uncertainty is particularly high and the possible impact on the sector or the organization is potentially significant.

In *step four*, we develop four rudimentary but equally plausible or probable future scenarios. Each of these scenarios will be elaborated in further detail during the subsequent steps. After a new group debate, we work on these scenarios in *step five* until we have created narrative stories that sketch possible futures.

*Step six* consists of identifying the signs or signals for which we must remain alert, because they point us towards evolutions leading in the direction of one of the four plausible future scenarios.

In *step seven*, we test our proposed strategy or the strategic decisions in the various possible future environments.

In *step eight* we formulate our recommendations. In *step nine* we make a well-documented and clear report. *Step 10* is monitoring and control. In this final step we systematically monitor the environment to detect changes or variations from our signposts.

Here is a list of the ten steps of the road map:

1.  Interviewing of experts: the identification of internal and external issues that affect the core question, strategic issue or problem;

2.  Identification of the key drivers;

3.  Selecting and choosing the key uncertainties;

4.  Development of the scenario matrix with two key uncertainties;

5.  Description of the scenarios;

6.  Selection of signposts;

7.  Testing of the strategy for each scenario;

8.  Strategic options and recommendations;

9.  Presentation of the final report;

10. Monitoring signposts and report variations.

Figure 12 graphically illustrates these ten steps in a flowchart. We will go through each of the steps in more detail but first it may be useful to describe the purpose of this method in a business context. The broad lines of the roadmap remain valid for other applications, although some adjustments may be needed. In our example, the aim of the exercise is to test the strategy of an organization. The exact purpose of the exercise is therefore:

- To gain insight into the long-term future, based on specific strategic questions;
- To qualify and quantify the main risks and opportunities, as well as the strengths and weaknesses of the organization;
- To identify new strategic orientations, options and actions to improve and preserve profitability in the long term;
- To develop signposts for the management, which will help to detect significant changes in the environment that will lead to a change of scenario and hence strategy.

**Figure 12: Strategic scenario planning**

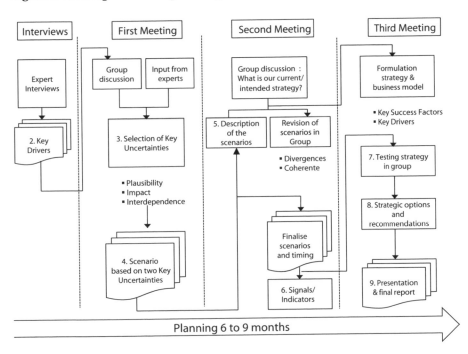

© *Gosselin D.P. 2006-2016.*

- We will now follow the flow chart in Figure 12 to work through the steps of a typical scenario exercise in detail:

## Step 1: Interviewing of experts

We first need to identify the discussion points that affect our focal question, using interviews and desk research. During the interviews, we try to identify all possible factors: constraints, stakeholders, trends, *etc.*, which may have an impact on the future strategic challenges related to our focal question.

In order to map out all possible factors, the core team conducts dozens of interviews with *remarkable people*: different experts with a vision on future issues and evolutions in the domains affecting the focal question. The objective is to understand and document the views of these remarkable people about the future in their field of competence. When selecting remarkable people, it is important to choose experts who are outspoken, unusual or who have extreme positions in the debate. At this stage, we are not looking for a consensus, but rather for logical arguments and visions that give us dispersion in terms of possible future evolutions. It is essential that these interviews:

- Try to find out about the *distant future*: the horizon is between five and fifty years. In this way, it is possible to transcend current day-to-day problems and competitive tensions, allowing fundamental challenges to become evident;
- Look at the *future environment*: the broad economic, cultural, political, social, ecological, technological and international environment in which the future will unfold.

Both these elements are important: the focus must reach far enough into the future and the factors to be assessed must be situated in the *contextual environment*, not in the transactional environment. When in doubt about the relevant environment, there is a *simple criterion* that can be applied: (a) can an individual player influence the environmental factor? If so, we are dealing with a transactional environment, which should be avoided; (b) is the influence of an individual player limited or non-existent? If so, we are dealing with a contextual environment, on which the interview should focus. Avoid and resist at all times the gravitational force of the contemporary, the current, the short term and the near future.

Experts who should be interviewed in an exercise to define a corporate or business strategy include:

- People within your own organization with a vision of the future;
- Leading editors of specialized magazines for your industry;
- Leading companies in your sector;
- Leading customers in your sector;
- Prominent academics in your industry;
- Prominent experts in your field.

The questions put to the interviewees must gauge that person's individual vision of the future. Some typical examples include:

- What in your opinion is the most important question facing us in the future (horizon: 10-15 years)?
- What are the three main trends that could change industry and society during this period?
- How do you see the sector developing in ten, fifteen and twenty years' time (and why)?
- What are the three main uncertainties (which you can already see now) and how will these evolve in the future (and why)?
- What do you see as the three main challenges in the sector in ten to fifteen years' time (and why)?
- What will be the critical success factors in the future? In other words: who will be the winners and losers (and why)?

In addition to making a transcript of the interviews for further analysis (it can be interesting if some elements are repeated in several different interviews), it is recommended to immediately write a summary of the prominent themes put forward by the interviewee as being important for the development of your future vision.

## Step 2: Identifying the key drivers

In the second step, the interviews are used (if necessary in combination with additional desk research support) to prepare a *long list* of key uncertainties and key drivers.

Key uncertainties and key drivers are those *contextual factors* or combinations of factors that can have a significant impact on the sector in which the organization intends to be active in the future. This is the case even if the evolution of some of those drivers is still uncertain today. For example, climate change will play a key role as a driver for change in both the energy and transport sectors, although we are still not certain about the impact it will have. Similarly, demographics and (in particular) aging populations will be a driver of change in the health sector, while new technologies will drive change in almost every sector.

In this step, all the drivers that might possibly affect the sector must be identified and listed, without forming a judgment. Judgment forming will be discussed later. The main objective at this stage is to make as good an inventory as possible of potential drivers and uncertainties for the future.

Using this inventory of drivers and uncertainties as input, a first plenary session should be organized. By 'plenary session' we mean a first discussion with a group composed of the scenario team members who carried out the interviews and the desk research, supplemented by additional experts, specialists, mangers or stakeholders involved in the strategic scenario exercise.

## Step 3: Selecting and choosing the key uncertainties (first plenary meeting)

The purpose of the first plenary meeting is to select and prioritize the preliminary findings from the interviews and desk research. This process of selection and prioritization occurs during extended group discussions and debates. The selection is made from the previously compiled *long list* of key uncertainties and key drivers (*cf.* contextual factors) with a significant impact on the future performance of the organization and its industry. This is done by positioning each of these factors on a two dimensional matrix called an *impact/uncertainty matrix* (I/U matrix), as shown in Figure 13.

On the horizontal x-axis, we put the level of *uncertainty* or ignorance of a factor (*i.e.* a key uncertainty or key driver); on the vertical y-axis, we position the *potential (future) impact* of a factor. The higher a factor scores on the y-axis, the greater its future potential impact on the organization and its industry. The higher a factor scores on the x-axis, the greater the uncertainty that the factor will occur. Using this process, all factors are eventually positioned on the matrix.

**Figure 13: The impact/uncertainty matrix**

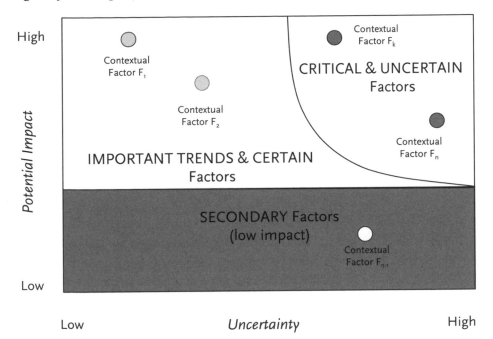

*Source*: based on Van der Heijden (2005).

Factors located on the lower part of the y-axis are *secondary factors*. They will always have a low impact, whether they occur or not (*cf*. $F_{n-1}$). As such, they can be ignored.

Factors located on the upper part of the y-axis must be treated differently. They are important because of their potential impact. High potential impact factors with a high certainty to occur are often identifiable and can be detected as short-term *trends*, hence explaining their low level of uncertainty (*cf*. $F_1$, $F_2$). The most important factors, however, are the factors in the right upper corner of the matrix, which combine a high level of uncertainty with a high level of impact. These are the *critical and uncertain divers and uncertainties*. This is where we should place our focus (*cf*. $F_k...F_n$).

During this plenary session, the aim is to *make uncertainty explicit*. Through the use of the matrix, we are able to discuss and debate risks, uncertainties and assumptions in a structured way. This allows us to concentrate on the most important factors. Using an I/U matrix, we can actually reduce the complexity of the situation. By so doing, we avoid confused discussions about multiple, non-weighted, potential impact drivers and uncertainties. It is during these debates that we are able for the first time to raise issues that were often hidden or even unknown before (*cf.* mathematical modelling, extrapolations and projections, where uncertainties, hypotheses and assumptions often remain hidden or are not explicitly mentioned).

Another essential point that needs to be addressed during this first plenary session is the *mutual interdependence* of the various factors on the I/U matrix. It is nearly always possible to reduce or cluster the key factors down to a workable number, since they are often mutually correlated or connected. Imagine that 'the aging of the population' and 'the future scarcity of young labour' are both on the *long list*. These are clearly two sides of the same phenomenon: the aging of the population is directly related to the scarcity of young labour, so one clustered driver – *e.g.* 'ageing' – can replace both.[55]

## Step 4: Developing a scenario matrix with two key uncertainties

Before the end of the first plenary session, another key decision must be made: the choice of the two most important key drivers. This choice is determined using the I/U matrix and by considering:

- Which two factors cause the greatest uncertainty?
- Which two factors have the greatest potential impact on the organization and its industry?

Because we are limiting ourselves to two dominant drivers, it is necessary to make sure that they are independent or *orthogonal*.[56]

Inexperienced users of the strategic scenario method often show a lack of understanding of the process and ask some basic and fundamental questions, such as:

- Isn't the choice of just two key drivers potentially risky?
- Might we not neglect other essential factors?
- Why is it not possible to work more exhaustively and use all drivers?

The reason for this restriction is the need to *reduce the complexity*. This is crucial, because otherwise the human mind cannot function meaningfully (*cf.* bounded rationality). With three or more key drivers, everything becomes too complicated for our brains. Strategy and strategic thinking is the art of reducing complexity without losing sight of the essential. Besides, there is a guarantee for those who fear that key factors will be missed by applying the stringent selection criterion of only two drivers: at a later stage, all the other identified drivers will also be discussed during the logical reasoning process used to develop the narrative description of the different scenarios. For the time being, it is important to trust the method: no insights will be lost if the method is rigorously applied.

Having made our choice, the next step is to differentiate or polarize the two key drivers to the extreme. We make the first driver highly negative as well as positive, by placing it on a bipolar axis. Imagine that our organization has come to the conclusion during the plenary meeting that the 'price of oil' is the first key driver influencing the industry (*i.e.* the contextual environment); that there is great uncertainty about the price of oil in the future; and that this can have a potentially huge impact on the organization. We can polarize this 'price of oil' on an axis by specifying an extremely low price of oil at one end and an extremely high price at the other end.

Next, we do the same for the second key driver. Suppose we have concluded that it is possible to produce sub-Saharan solar energy and to transport it worldwide through superconductors at an ambient temperature. Our second key driver might then be, for example, 'the cost to produce and distribute solar energy from the sub-Sahara on a worldwide scale'. Since both the identified key drivers are cost-related and depend on the maturity of innovation and the acceptance or use of the technology, they can vary between very low and very high costs or prices. In this way, both the key drivers become bipolar variables. As we have previously checked that both drivers are independent[57] variables and hence *orthogonal*, we can present them on two perpendicular axes. As a result, we get four combinations and four possible scenarios (Figure 14).

**Figure 14: The scenario matrix**

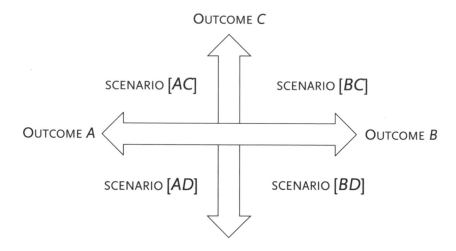

At this point, it is useful to briefly describe the final status of the four scenarios. Each scenario should then be given a catchy and appropriate name, which is short, indicative and objective. Try to avoid long and difficult names. To bring this first plenary session to a close, try to formulate the most important questions that each scenario evokes.

## Step 5: Description of the scenarios (second plenary session)

The second plenary session demands far more preparation. It is during this second meeting that we test the *actual or intended strategy* and *business model* of the organization. This requires that we accurately describe and justify the possible future worlds of each of the four scenario quadrants (Figure 14). This enables us to get a clear picture of each scenario, in order to stimulate discussion and debate, so that we can further improve and enhance our understanding and eventually develop narrative scenario descriptions, including the identification of signposts.

To describe each scenario of each quadrant, we need to take the key drivers (*cf. long list*) and order them in successive logical steps to form a plausible and coherent environment. For each of the four scenarios, we use the orthogonal primary variables in each quadrant as the starting point to construct a comprehensive reasoning. We then use the other 'secondary' drivers as building blocks to further strengthen the internal consistency and coherence of our logical steps. The guiding principles to develop these logical sequences of steps, which together make up the scenario narrative or *story*, are the questions we framed for each scenario in step five. Subsequently, we bring additional structure to each scenario, so as to avoid internal inconsistencies. We do this by focusing on the interdependencies of the variables, by building on the relationships between the variables, and by focusing on the potential interactions that have emerged during our previous investigations. Finally, we need to verify that each scenario story is reliable, coherent and cohesive.

Scenarios are only credible and useful if they meet the five criteria proposed by Michel Godet:[58] (1) *plausibility*, (2) *credibility*, (3) *coherence*, (4) *relevance* and (5) *transparency*. Or to use the words of Nicolas Boileau (1636-1711), who wrote in 1674 in his book *L'Art Poétique*: "*What is conceived well is expressed clearly, and the words to say it arrive with ease.*" The main objective is to make well-conceived, plausible, credible and consistent stories, as if they were "vivid memories from the future".


## Step 6: Selecting signposts

Within the information we receive every day, there are hidden signals that announce movement towards a possible reality, corresponding to a particular scenario. Or to put it another way: when we have reached the future and look back at the past, we often think: "*How is it possible that we did not see this future coming? There were a lot of signals that pointed in this direction*". Afterwards, it is easy to explain the future by looking at the past. Most of the time, we do not see these signals and signs in advance, because there are simply too many options for the future to develop: we cannot place this information in the broader context of a possible future. We have, as it were, *no memory of the future* that triggers our memory in the present. However, once a future has developed and choices have been made, the path followed is easy to explain. This backward reasoning gives us the impression that we could have – and perhaps should have – easily foreseen the future. However, this is mostly an illusion; in reality, it is virtually impossible for rapidly changing and complex environments. The complexity involved in predicting the future is many times more complex than explaining the future after it has happened: the future is asymmetric in information compared to the present, but because we can easily explain the past, we have the illusion we can predict the future.

A good illustration of this is the recent reports that talk about the Indians, who have made it their mission to go to the moon. It was placed in the newspaper under the *faits divers* section.

*The strong economic growth of India has been accompanied by an insatiable hunger for raw materials and energy. Taking into consideration the scarcity of fossil fuel energy and the volatility of the prices, this uncertainty weighs heavily on the country's future. However, an alternative option was raised during a strategic scenario exercise: exploration of the moon. Samples of minerals derived from the moon contain an abundant amount of helium-3 ($He_3$), a variant of the gas that we know from its use in refrigerators and hot air balloons. When helium-3 combines with heavy hydrogen ($H_2$ deuterium), a fusion reaction with a huge amount of energy is created. 25 tons of helium – the amount that can be transported in a space shuttle – is enough to fulfil the electricity needs of the U.S. for one year! In 2004, the former President of India, Abdul Kalam, declared at an International Conference on the Exploitation of the Moon that this arid celestial body contains one million tons of helium-3 – an amount containing ten times more energy than all fossil fuels still remaining on earth together. True, the reactor technology to turn helium-3 into energy is still in its infancy. At the current rate of technological progress, this development will take another thirty years. Although, according to scientists, this can be accelerated if there is more funding and focus.*

The Indian *faits divers* to go to the moon suddenly has a greater meaning in this context. It is a signpost that leads to a scenario in which a first transport from the moon to earth could already take place by 2020-2025. The future is closer than we think![59]

How can we capture the signals that point in the direction of a particular scenario? Which signals are already obvious?

We need a plan to detect these signals or signposts actively, we need an *early warning system* (EWS). During the second plenary meeting, it is necessary to discuss which signals we should monitor for each scenario and how this will be organized.

## Step 7: Testing the strategy (third plenary meeting)

We now have four scenarios, four possible future worlds, which sketch an environment in which we can test a strategy and a business model. In the terminology of strategic scenario thinking, we speak of *wind tunnelling*. This is an analogy with the extensive testing that a prototype of a plane (*cf.* strategy or business model) undergoes in a simulated wind tunnel. This tests the robustness of the design in various extreme wind conditions (*cf.* the scenarios). Such a test can be done in several ways:

- The basic strategy or business model can be tested against the extreme scenarios;
- A SWOT[60] analysis can be made for the different scenarios. Note that here we are using the SWOT testing on possible *future* scenarios. It is actually nonsense to do a SWOT analysis for the current environment of an organization, although this is often a common error made by many organizations;
- We can identify *first movers* or organizations that respond and invest in the belief that a particular scenario will actually come true;
- We can identify strategic shortcomings in the light of one or other of the scenarios. This involves the identification of domains in which innovations should be sought;
- We can identify which scenarios, relationships, alliances or partnerships can be useful;
- We can identify with whom proactive commitments can best be made.

## Step 8: Identifying strategic options and making recommendations

This step involves the identification of the main implications for each of the scenarios. The SWOT analysis is a good basis for this: from the strengths and weaknesses of the organization in each scenario and the opportunities and threats that currently exist in the transactional environment of the organization, the implications and options become well-defined and precise. The analysis of options can be done using the following questions:

- What is needed to stimulate the strengths-opportunities couples in each scenario?
- What can be done to avoid the weaknesses-threats couples?

This method brings out a range of strategic options for each scenario. The options that are common to all scenarios are the 'no-brainers': the conclusions are obvious. The options that are not common to the different scenarios demand that choices be made. At this point, we need to list the key or critical choices, which require a deeper and a more profound understanding.

## Step 9: Presenting the final report

At some point, we must present a final report. The big advantage of fixing a report date is that it sets a deadline for the project. If the report is presented in a sufficiently lively and creative manner, it can also inspire a broader group of stakeholders. It is, however, a misapprehension to think that the full wealth of insights generated during the scenario building exercise can be transferred to people who only read the final report – although this is nothing new. Reports continue to be just reports and are therefore of limited value in the learning process. We must ensure that key people (*i.e.* key decision-makers or influencers) are included in the strategic foresight exercise from the early stages or are closely involved with the core team. In this way, we can at least be certain that they have experienced or been exposed to the entire learning process. Afterwards, this will prove to be strategically extremely valuable and help to create the basis for a strategic sustainable competitive advantage : increasing the future decision and implementation speed.

## Step 10: Monitoring and control

---

*During the year 2006, the world's attention was focused on Thailand. After days of protests and street violence, the impossible happened. During the visit of Prime Minister Thaksin Shinawatra to the United Nations on Tuesday 19 September 2006, a group of soldiers drove out the government, arrested ministers, accused Thaksin of corruption, cancelled the scheduled elections of 15 October 2006, declared the constitution temporarily invalid, dissolved parliament, forbade political activity and censored the media. The army made Rama IX (i.e. the ninth king) Bhumibol the Great head of state and promised new elections and the return to democracy later.*
*The executive committee of a global company with significant local investments and a stock market listing in Thailand immediately called an emergency meeting.*

*A teleconference was set up to discuss the possible options. Although this meeting was hastily organized when the news of the coup was heard, the executive board members already had some information to hand. In fact, these events, as they occurred in Thailand, were similar, but not identical, to a scenario they had developed almost two years earlier. During these strategic conversations and interpretation debates (i.e. sensemaking), both local management from Thailand and the senior management of the group from the headquarters in Europe had been present. In this way, when the crisis broke out they all spoke the same language and they all understood the relationship between cause-impact-action (CIA). This meant that after the outbreak of the coup, they did not need to waste time analysing the Thai political environment, or estimating the impact or preparing required actions. This had already been done. Above all, they did not need to waste time explaining all of this to corporate senior executives, including their advisors at corporate headquarters, working in a different time zone and too far away to be more than superficially involved in this 'glocal' (global and local) reality.*

---

Research into the use of the strength-weakness analysis in strategy has shown that decision-makers see more risks than opportunities when they are confronted with a non-trusted environment or when they are too far away from the problem. They overestimate their own weaknesses and they underestimate their strengths. Frequently, top managers and political leaders look for interpretations outside their organization or quickly ask the advice of people they have confidence in: professors, consultants, corporate bankers, friends or even, in some extreme cases, fortune tellers. Research also shows that at these moments leaders have more faith in external sources than in internal sources, even at the risk of following nothing more than rumours. The reason for this? They are afraid of manipulation by subordinates and colleagues. *Power makes people blind and stupid.*

The Thai example also illustrates something else: a process of strategic conversations, based on scenario thinking, required the leadership of the organization to think about possible future developments. This made them more alert for signals that indicated a trend towards one or other of the scenarios. This proactive mindfulness leverages many times over the alertness of management for weak signals, making them less surprised by dramatic events – certainly in comparison with leaders who have not thought about possible long-term evolutions. These latter leaders are less able to recognize and make sense of weak signals. They have a restricted *memory of the future* – and this makes a world of difference, as the Thai example illustrates.

## Applying the scenario method

**Figure 15: The use of strategic scenario thinking**

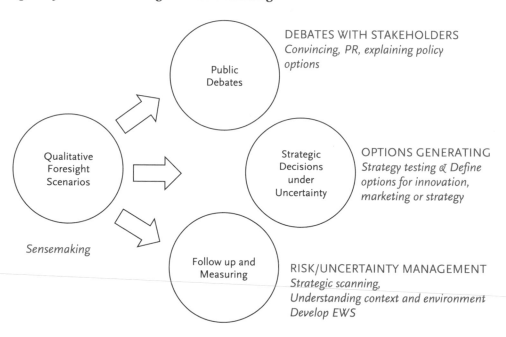

The ten-step process to apply strategic scenario thinking as outlined above is perhaps more appropriate to a business or political context, and is particularly concerned with the key question: what is the context in which we should test our strategy or policy? Of course, each project has its own characteristics and priorities.

**Table 5: The use of the scenario method**

| Type/Description | Objective |
|---|---|
| Decision-making scenarios | Testing of decisions for robustness |
| Normative scenarios | Pushing a community towards a specific perspective |
| Dialogue between communities, problem solving, conflict | Commitment of leading community to explore future management options |
| Align policy | Facilitation of various ministries to attune policies |
| Align organization and engagement | Provide an overarching focus for strategic conversations and alignment within the organization and strategic support for organizational development |
| Environmental scanning | Allow the organization to learn about – and take a position on – specific assumptions on which the strategy is based |
| Scenario-based thinking | A way of thinking, embedded in all decision-making processes or choices |
| Leadership coaching with scenarios | Promoting personal research on which to base personal strategies |

*Source*: based on Van der Merwe (2008).

This means that the attention devoted to each step will differ from project to project. The application of the method will therefore vary according to the nature and objective of the scenario exercise. Figure 15 and Table 5 give a brief overview of possible uses of scenarios. This use will depend on the field of application (*e.g.* politics, marketing, strategy, new product development, risk assessment, *etc.*), the type of key questions that need to be answered, and the objectives to be achieved by using strategic scenario planning.

A very different application is *political futures thinking*: a dialogue between communities in order to solve conflicts. The broad lines of the roadmap, as described above for a corporate context, remain valid, although the process might differ to reflect the social context. We can illustrate this political/social application briefly, without describing each step in detail, by examining a case in which the scenario method led to a historical success: the Mont Fleur scenarios.

## The Mont Fleur scenarios: the wisdom of futures thinking

South Africa, early 1990. The country is plagued by brutal violence and major uncertainty. The first democratic elections must still take place. After more than 27 years in prison, Nelson Mandela is released on 11 February of that year. He promises a widespread national programme in accordance with the economic politics of the *African National Congress* (ANC). The opposition parties are legalized, including the radical black *Pan African Congress* (PAC), which has not yet officially given up the armed struggle and has declared that the help of the Chinese Liberation Army should be enlisted to overthrow the regime! Predicting what the future will bring in such circumstances is extremely hazardous. Even so, in 1990 major historical questions urgently needed to be answered. Above all: how can South Africa leave behind *apartheid* and prepare for a better future?

That, in a nutshell, was the situation, the problem and the opportunity: *how to manage a transitional period that could reconcile the many antagonistic views and prepare for a better future without plunging the country into chaos?* Political parties, trade unions, business leaders, academics and government all had an opinion. They all wanted to influence the future and they all wanted something different.

At the same time, the German Friedrich Ebert Stiftung offered Professor Pieter Le Roux of the University of the Western Cape the necessary means to organise a conference on the future of South Africa. Le Roux was sceptical about the chances of success. In those days, there were many conferences and forums, but their 'recommendations' usually fell on deaf ears, because the participants merely recited their own well-known and firmly held positions. Professor Le Roux decided to opt for another approach: future thinking based on the scenario method.

Le Roux brought representatives of all the relevant parties – about 22 people – together for three weekends at the Mont Fleur Hotel[61], a seminar centre in the *Blaauwklippen Valley* on the outskirts of Stellenbosch. The participants were invited personally, not as representatives of their organization. The hotel is a 45 minute drive from Cape Town, nestling between the vineyards and the *fynbos* (i.e. the typical vegetation in the Cape region of thin, spindly trees and bushes, hence the Dutch name *fynbos* meaning 'thin forest'). For many South Africans, the name Mont Fleur has become synonymous with the historical developments that led the country away from *apartheid* in a peaceful transition.

The participants at the seminar had to examine how the country could be prepared for a new future:

> *"How can we adapt to what could happen and not to what each participant wants to happen?"*

In other words, the scenario thinking method was introduced to answer just a single question: according to the participants, what could conceivably happen during the next ten years (*i.e.* from 1992 till 2002)?

The Canadian Adam Kahane[62] was asked to join the discussions. During the early 1990s, Kahane was head of the social, political, economic and technological scenarios for Royal Dutch Shell in London. He was brought to South Africa for his expertise in solving complex problems involving many stakeholders. Kahane never returned to Shell afterwards.[63]

In the following months, a series of logical, plausible and consistent stories were developed about what might happen in the next decade in the form of four scenarios. Each scenario explained how events would unfold and develop over the years 1992-2002.

The *ostrich scenario* told the story of a fully white, non-representative government that against all odds continues to put its head in the sand by failing to honour negotiated agreements with the black majority.

The *lame duck scenario* anticipated a weak government that attempts to meet everyone's requirements during a long transition period but eventually leaves everyone disappointed.

The *flight-of-the-flamingos scenario* described a successful transition whereby the government develops a sustainable policy that puts the country on a path to inclusive growth and democracy. In short, a scenario in which the different parties converge gradually towards each other in accordance with a consistent and wise policy.

In the fourth scenario, the *Icarus scenario*, a black government comes to power. Blinded by the euphoria of finally achieving executive power and armed with noble intentions, it embarks on a populist economic policy that seeks to eradicate poverty as quickly as possible, using public spending as its tool. This, of course, derails the public finances and leads to a collapse of the economy, with resultant public dissatisfaction. The participants talked openly about the risk that such a left-wing policy entailed (*cf.* "*while all of them were left-wing oriented.*"[64]). This government would have been just like Icarus, who flew too near the sun and burnt his wings, bringing him crashing down to earth with a bump...

The Mandela Government eventually decided to adopt a cautious economic policy, which was a surprise for friend and foe alike. As a result, the much-feared economic crash did not take place – and all thanks to the Mont Fleur scenarios!

In July 1992, the scenarios were published in a 14-page document. A 30-minute video was also produced, in which cartoons were combined with presentations by the team members. The final report was distributed as a free supplement in the South African newspaper *The Weekly Mail & The Guardian Weekly*. In this way, the team members were able to discuss the scenarios with more than 50 groups, including political parties, trade unions, companies, academics and civil rights organizations.

Perhaps these scenarios seem of little relevance for the reader today. But in 1992, they reflected the fundamental choices that South Africa had to make in a context characterized by huge ideological differences between all the parties involved. Scenario thinking brought possible futures to life. Some of them were not desirable; others would lead to disappointment; only one scenario gave hope for a better future – and, fortunately, that was the scenario that was chosen.

What was the contribution of this Mont Fleur scenarios thinking? A first result is that this scenario exercise actually created a common understanding and a shared language about the future at a very critical time. This made it possible to conduct strategic conversations with a much broader public than just the elite around the negotiating table. To illustrate: a preacher spoke about *flamingos* during Sunday mass. A listener phoned a radio programme to express concern about the *lame duck*. Frederik Willem de Klerk, leader of the National Party, once said: "*I'm no ostrich.*" Tito Mboweni, governor of the South African Central Bank at the time, stated in his inaugural speech in 1999: "*We are not Icarus. There is no reason to fear that we will fly too close to the sun.*"

A second result of the Mont Fleur exercise was the creation of informal networks between the participants. Apparently, the groundwork for the formal negotiations and critical agreements was made in this way. The group that came together in 1991 in the middle of the chaos now reads like a 2016 Who's Who of South Africa, with names such as Tito Mboweni, Trevor Manuel, Christo Wiese, Vincent Maphai, Saki Macozoma and others.

The third and final result is perhaps the least tangible, but also the most fundamental: by thinking about the unthinkable (*i.e.* a failure of the transition), problems that could not be discussed before now became discussable. Before the Mont Fleur meetings, there were no words and no names for the phenomena and the fears. It was impossible to talk openly about them. *Strategic conversations* changed all this – and changed the destiny of a nation.

The path that South Africa has followed since 1992 is most comparable to the 'flight of the flamingos', although it is far from identical. But by creating openness for a variety of possible and plausible futures, the minds of the participants were influenced and the Mont Fleur-process contributed to the current results. Things could have been very different – and most likely much worse.

However, the lesson of this story lies not in the ultimate outcome. Its tremendous value lies in the *process*. It characterizes one of the most important innovations in the political transition of South Africa: the development of a method of dialogue that can deal with complex situations involving numerous stakeholders. Since 1992, South Africa has applied this method in hundreds of informal forums on many different policy issues. The country still suffers from major problems, but the successful transition fundamentally contributed to making South Africa what it is today: the long time main growth region and a source of hope for the entire African continent.

Isn't there a lesson to be learned from this approach in South Africa for Europe, Ukraine, Belgium or even your country? We leave it to the reader to decide.

# Summary

1.  The key to understanding the future lies deeper than the top of the iceberg that is visible on the surface: the real key is in understanding the structure, the systems and the causality of relationships and their combinations and effects. The answers to these matters lie hidden under the surface. This requires attention to the interpretation process, which is called *sensemaking*. The scenario method creates a forum in which decision-makers can explore this structural level of different forces and their combinations.

2.  In practice, a scenario thinking process takes place in accordance with a road-map. For a project supporting a business strategy, the 10 steps of the roadmap might be:

    -   Interviewing experts
    -   Identifying key drivers
    -   Filtering and choosing key uncertainties
    -   Developing the scenario matrix with two key uncertainties
    -   Description of the scenarios
    -   Selecting signposts
    -   Testing the strategy
    -   Agreeing strategic options and making recommendations
    -   Presenting the final report
    -   Monitoring and follow-up

3.  Future thinking and, more in particular, the strategic scenario thinking method also has many other applications; namely, those in which a dialogue between communities is pursued to resolve conflicts and problems. We can illustrate this social application with the historical success of the method in developing the Mont Fleur scenarios.

4.  The Mont Fleur scenarios: what lessons can your country or your project draw from this?

5.  How can a board of directors or a board of governors use strategic scenario or foresight methods to organise and stimulate strategic conversations? How can we secure the method a higher place on the management agenda, so that it receives much more attention from decision-makers?

# Chapter 6
# Uncertain futures need future thinking

*"Ce qui est nécessaire n'est jamais ridicule."*[65]
Cardinal de Retz (1613-1679)

A large number of companies, enterprises, organizations, regions and nations now try to deal more actively with the future as an unpredictable and uncertain environment, necessitating better methods of preparation. Consequently, they build competence in future(s) thinking through different approaches and different applications of strategic conversations on a more or less permanent basis. The culture and the processes to master and adopt future thinking represent a major competitive advantage both to businesses and countries in highly uncertain times.

Firstly, identifying problems and responding with decisive action can all happen much faster if organizations have already discussed the possible strategic options within the framework of multiple scenario thinking.

Secondly, this type of thinking encourages a higher degree of delegation, promotes the development of strategic vision, brings to light hidden assumptions, facilitates a consensus between the several parties involved and, last but not least, offers a perspective and point of view on difficult problems.

Thirdly, it protects organizations and countries more effectively against unexpected events and it focuses leadership attention where it is most critically needed.

In short, future(s) thinking lays the foundations for a *learning organization*. This is the central concept in recent strategic thinking in terms of elaborating survival strategies in rapidly changing or turbulent environments.

In this chapter we will discuss in more depth what the future might bring in the next decade: in other words, we will look at future trends and challenges. We will make a plea to introduce future(s) thinking as a complementary scientific method for policy-making in both private and public organizations. We will seek to justify this approach by giving a brief overview of a number of different initiatives currently active in the world today.

## Future trends and grand challenges

Which environmental factors will contribute in the coming decades to an increase in risk, uncertainty or turbulence? Some evolutions and trends are predictable to some extent, whereas others can only be estimated. We also need to consider the plausible environmental factors. To do this, we will start by listing a number of important uncertainty factors derived from the contextual environment and discuss how their interdependencies can cause turbulence. But remember: these provisional conclusions are neither predictions nor future scenarios!

So where should we begin our *grand tour* of trends and challenges for the 21st century? In view of developments in recent decades, the fields of technology, public finance, demography, climate change, scarce natural resources, ecology and migration seem like a logical place to start. Because of their interconnectedness, they can all cause turbulence.

If we extrapolate current technology trends, we may plausibly expect the following:

- The limits of computer calculating capacity have still not been reached. This has an effect on many different applications in many different domains (*cf.* big data). Some internet entrepreneurs, like the Belgian Peter Hinssen, speak of the *new normal* when referring to digitization claiming that the majority of computer applications and their possible impact on society still have to be invented, developed and assessed;
- Personal communication on ultrafast broadband computer networks will perhaps become a reality within the next decade;[66]
- The further development of robotics, nanotechnology and 3D printing will allow us to produce buildings, factories and products using robots (perhaps even on different celestial bodies, as planned by NASA);
- The coming decades will see a strong increase in life expectancy,[67] encouraged

by a combination of the above technological advancements. Does this seem like *science fiction?* Just think back in time, let's say 20 years ago. If you had predicted then that by 2016 there would be such things as broadband internet, Google, Facebook, cell phones and smart phones such as the *iPhone*™, *iWatch*™, *iPad*™, *Galaxy*™, and Wi-Fi, people would have said that you were crazy. None of these things existed in 1996. And some of them are already almost obsolete! Such is the pace of modern change.

Yet the extrapolation of technology trends is nothing compared to the complexity of trying to anticipate future changes in the social and geopolitical context. Governments and companies alike will be faced with huge social and geopolitical challenges in the decades to come. They must safeguard both availability and access to sufficient food, energy, water and raw materials for an increasing, ageing, better educated and more empowered population. At the same time, they have to prevent the calamities inherent in climate change, social breakdown and mass migration – and all on a global scale. Talk about a challenge.

Huge resources will be needed to tackle these problems, which leads us to another complication. Many countries in Europe and the western world are already facing massive public debt deficits. As a result, the welfare state and the role of the government will be seriously questioned in the years ahead. This is already happening in Belgium, France, Greece, Italy and Spain.

Since the mid-19th century, modern Western governments have taken on an ever larger packet of tasks and powers. The funding of these new responsibilities was only possible through an increase in *public debt* – also referred to as *national, state, sovereign or government debt* – since incoming tax revenues were not sufficient to cover all the associated additional costs (mainly relating to pensions and health care). Gradually, the limits of this type of government model have been reached, since in practice it is almost impossible to control these debts. What's more, nearly every country in the West (except for the U.S.) already have tax rates that are among the highest in the world, in combination with the highest levels of public debt (Attali, 2010, OCDE 2015).

Table 6 shows the trend in indebtedness over a period of 10 years for the seven most indebted countries in the world. Indebtedness is measured by the ratio: *public debt* divided by *gross domestic product* (GDP). This is the so-called *debt-to-GDF ratio*. In each of the seven countries, the debt-to-GDP ratio in 2014 is higher than in 2004. Moreover, the lowest ratio for each country during the 10-year period all occurred in 2004. Table 6 therefore not only reveals that public debt of these governments is high, but also indicates that the trend is consistently upwards.

During the period 2013-2015, the E.U. has broadly managed to stabilize the debt-to-GDP ratio at around 100%. The figure for the U.S. also hovers around 100%, but this represents a significant increase in just a few years time.

**Table 6: The trend in indebtedness of the most indebted nations**

| Country | Debt-to-GDP Ratio (%) | |
| --- | --- | --- |
| | 2004 | 2014 |
| Japan | 165.6 | 227.2 |
| Greece | 98.6 | 175.1 |
| Italy | 103.9 | 132.6 |
| Portugal | 57.6 | 129.0 |
| Singapore | 98.0 | 105.5 |
| United States | 61.0 | 103.2 |
| Belgium | 94.2 | 101.5 |

*Source*: Eurosat, ECB, IMF, CIA, Federal Reserve Bank, OECD.

In early 2015, the U.S. total public debt amounted to $18 trillion,[68] in comparison with 'just' $11.9 trillion in 2009. This represents roughly 1000% of annual U.S. tax revenue in an economy that is not used to or encouraged to save. Since the 2008 banking crisis, interest rates have plummeted, reaching historical low levels by 2016. Of the countries listed in Table 6, the U.S. has the highest short-term government interest rate at 0.25%; Singapore's rate is at 0.17%; the four European countries at 0.05%; and at one point the Japanese rate was actually at 0.00%! Even the Bank of England, founded as long ago as July 1694, was forced in 2015 to drop it long-term interest rate below 2% for the first time in its 320 year history. Long-term rates throughout the rest of the E.U. and in the U.S. are also below 1%.

The major financial and economic crisis of recent years, currently referred to as the 'Great Recession', started in 2007 and officially came to an end (according to economic theory) in 2009. The reality for the E.U. however, and to some extent for the U.S. as well, is that this recession has still not been contained by the time this book was written. Europe will most probably face years of continuing low growth combined with low inflation, the so-called *secular stagnation* (Teulings & Baldwin, 2014).[69] If this is the case, the E.U. – burdened as it is with high and increasing levels of social security expenditure (caused by demographic evolution), high rates of tax and high levels of indebtedness – could face a future that leads to a significant impoverishment of its population.

The *total public debt* is the total debt of the nation. It is partly owned by the government and partly owned by the public (*i.e.* by investors outside of government, including individuals, companies, corporations or foreign states). This means that the total public debt actually belongs to everyone and to no one. It is possible for a government to hand over this debt to the next duly elected government without any of its members feeling any sense of person responsibility for the deteriorating situation. Modern democratic governments, or at least some of the political parties that comprise them, have lived (and in some cases still live) under the delusion that a country cannot go bankrupt, because they assume they will always be able to continue borrowing money or raise taxes. Some rich countries do indeed have this luxury to some extent, but only under certain strict conditions, if they wish to maintain the prosperity of their population. And what are the conditions that allow membership to this exclusive club? It is not enough for countries to have strong economies and competent political leaders and governments; *they must also create and secure well-functioning institutions.* These were the findings of two world-class economists: Daron Acemoglu from the Massachusetts Institute of Technology and James A. Robinson from Harvard University (Acemoglu & Robinson, 2012). Well-functioning democratic institutions are one of the single most important factors explaining differences in wealth between nations. *It's the politics, stupid!*[70]

Most Western economies – particularly those in the E.U. countries – are today no longer able to maintain the level of their people's prosperity and meet their ever burgeoning welfare obligations without actually increasing their public debt! This means that the level of national productivity is no longer sufficient to pay for the level of social welfare and prosperity they once had. In this respect, there also seems to be a noticeable relationship between the growth of public debt and the degree of democratisation: the more democratic its government and their policies, the wealthier the nation and the higher its levels of public debt and taxation (*cf.* the Scandinavian countries). Given such a policy, particularly in combination with current demographic evolutions and an economic environment of secular stagnation, it seems almost certain that in the decades ahead public debt will continue to rise in both the E.U. and the U.S., unless countered by huge cuts in government expenditure. Even then, this course of action would seriously affect economic growth in both the short and medium term, imposing a need to further reduce expenditure or increase taxes, leading to *secular stagnation* and the impoverishment of its population. The situation in Greece in 2015 is a warning of what could happen in other E.U. countries if no solution is found. Trying to solve this *wicked problem* when we were suddenly confronted by it has definitely not worked. Futures thinking is perhaps a more appropriate way to approach the situation, but this calls for an institutional approach, implying the establishment of a new kind of planning policy bureau, or what we prefer to call an *Institute for the Future*.

In a context of globalisation, with increasing liberalization of goods and services, this poses an enormous socio-economic challenge in relation to competitiveness. If they wish to remain competitive, the richest countries with the highest debt-to-GDP ratios have the most to fear in terms of a loss of social protection and general prosperity. To make matters worse, after 2008 most E.U. countries, as well as the U.S., were forced to finance gigantic rescue operations to save their banking systems, in order to avoid an economic collapse that might ultimately have led to an economic depression. Eventually, governments will be required to repay this debt, either through savings or higher taxes, and most likely through both. Since 2012, political discussions within the E.U. have been focusing on this issue and seem likely to do so for some time. This has had the result of polarizing political debates between left wing liberal and right wing conservative solutions, pushing welfare and wealth distribution issues to the top of the political agenda. This is *the end* as foreseen in Francis Fukuyama's *The End of History* (Fukuyama, 1989) and the return – more than 25 years after the collapse of the Soviet Union – of the criticism of capitalism (Piketty, 2013).

An important part of the U.S. public debt – largely accumulated to pay the salaries of its countless officials, soldiers and researchers – is being financed with borrowed money from China.[71] In other words, money provided by poor Chinese workers, whose average monthly salary is less than $350,[72] roughly 50% of which is saved, are helping to finance the richest countries! When you consider startling facts of this kind, you start to understand the possible far-reaching consequences of *interactions* between the increasing role of the state, international finance and globalization. This complex and potentially dangerous situation calls for the need to *anticipate* and *foresee* possible evolutions. But the question remains: *do we have the appropriate tools?*

No doubt there are brilliant econometrists somewhere who will make the best possible estimates and forecasts of future evolutions based on ... an isolated macro-economic factor repeatedly estimated on the basis of historical data sets. Much the same method is used by company CFOs or financial specialists for budgeting purposes. This method is 'fine' – until it becomes clear that the future is not what they thought it would be! The problem is that they rarely or never consider combinations of interactions between the $L_{22}$ factors from the environment in their models. In complex and turbulent environments, this is a recipe for continuous – and usually unpleasant – surprises.

As an example, let us consider modelling the impact of demographic developments. After all by 2060, barring a nuclear war or a return of the bubonic plague, there will be considerably more of us than there are today.

Fifty years ago, there were roughly three billion people on earth; today, in 2016, we are currently with 7 billion. This is more than double the number of half a century ago. Perhaps by the middle of this century, there will be somewhere between 9 and 11 billion people, since we are currently growing at a rate of an additional 1 billion people every 14 years! By then, the concentration of the most important human capital will no longer be in Europe or in the U.S., but in Asia. The increase in world population will occur almost entirely in countries outside the OECD: 3 to 4 billion in India, China and the rest of Asia, while Africa is expected to increase by 1 billion, according to the most 'reliable' predictions. At the same time, the world population will also age significantly. Contrary to what is often thought, the ageing of population is not just a European problem: half of the world's population now lives in countries where the birth rate is below the mortality rate. This is why the population cannot remain in balance. Only Africa will remain relatively young and fertile, as to a lesser extent will South America.

You don't need to be a Malthusian genius to realize that these evolutions can provide a combination of factors and interactions that will ultimately bring turmoil. But which factors will be detected as weak signals by our governments? Will possible scenarios be thought through? Where and with whom do we have strategic conversations about these pressing problems?

And population is not our only worry. In the next 30 to 50 years, the world will probably become warmer than it is today. This is another crucial interaction factor. How many degrees will it warm up? This is a difficult question and the answer is scientifically difficult to estimate. Changes in rainfall patterns (rain, storm, snow) will most likely first affect those people who are least prepared to do something about it. They are also the ones who have least contributed to $CO_2$ emissions over the past 100 years. All current studies and analyses conclude that Africa will be hit hardest by climate change, and this is the continent were the population will plausibly increase by an additional 1 billion by 2050. Climate change will create an even greater challenge to providing food, energy and health care for all these people. But this same evolution can also have a major impact on European society. If global warming makes entire regions of Africa uninhabitable, mass migration to the 'old' continent becomes a distinct reality. Desertification already affects entire countries and whole regions, especially around the equator, leading to a growing exodus of the indigenous populations. Climate change, population growth and the reduction of impoverishment all combine to create a problem that can be characterized as the problem of *energy-water-food* – or EWF for short. It is unquestionably one of the most important and most urgent social and geopolitical grand challenges facing the world today. It not only concerns issues that are highly interconnected; they are also in competition with each other for possible solutions. The EWF relationship is clearly one of the great *wicked problems* of the 21st century.

**Figure 16: The Energy-Water-Food Nexus**

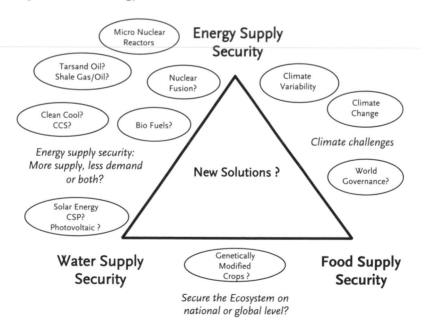

Figure 16 is a visual representation of this EWF relationship. The importance of adequate food and potable water requires little explanation. However, our prosperity also depends increasingly on availability and access to extensive energy networks, such as electricity. Developed countries have already reached such a level of energy dependency that people will start to die if a power interruption would last for longer than 35 days. Compared to our ancestors of 100 years ago, our modern and highly developed society is no longer able to survive without electricity: our refrigerators, heating, telephones, internet, computers, petrol pumps, signage, freezers, lighting, hospitals, *etc.* all work on electricity – and on the premise that it will continue to flow.

Once again: have all the possible scenarios been thought through? What factors do governments monitor as weak signals? Where are the strategic conversations relating to these problems? Where are the institutions that are supposed to deal with this?

Although our lives are becoming safer and healthier, it is also increasingly dependent on technology. Small problems can therefore have serious consequences. *Pandemics* are an example. As we live more and more in megacities, which do not all have the same technological infrastructure for waste treatment and health care, cauldrons of germs and diseases will form a growing risk for the entire world, partly due to the increase in international travel. Do you remember the Mexican flu[73] in 2009 or the super bacterium that had its origins in Indian sub-continent[74] or more recently the Ebola outbreak in and around the Niger delta in 2014? All had a worldwide impact.

The ecological challenge is therefore another major *wicked problem*. Unfortunately, we are consuming more than the planet can provide. Steady population growth combined with progress in education and development means that an increasing number of people aspire to higher levels of prosperity, often converted into higher levels of consumption. Today, the earth is just about capable of sustaining each of its 7 billion inhabitants, based on a maximum ecological footprint of 2.1 hectares per person, given the current state of technology and productivity. The reality, however, is that we are already consuming on average 2.7 hectares per person. In other words, we are eating away at the *natural resources* of the planet. These natural resources, formed over billions of years, are to a large extent irreplaceable. Before the end of the 21$^{st}$ century, we will most likely witness the end of the oil-based economy[75] and we will have to reduce our consumption of other raw materials by at least 40%. Or to put it differently: we must relearn how to save and to create surpluses. One interesting idea is that we may once again have to learn how to live with what the seasons offer us, as suggested by William McDonough and Michael Braungart in their 2002 book *Cradle to Cradle: remaking the way we make things.*

At the same time, we also face the challenge of reducing greenhouse gas (GHG) emissions (*i.e.* $CO_2$-equivalent gas emissions) by more than 80% between now and 2050, and possibly even achieve *negative emissions* of $CO_2$ (carbon dioxide) after that date. Amazingly, it was as long ago as 1896 that Svante August Arrhenius (1859-1927) formulated his *greenhouse law*,[76] postulating the relationship between $CO_2$ and climate, and even predicting that emissions of $CO_2$ from the burning of fossil fuels were large enough to cause global warming. Current climate models show a strong correlation between the concentration of GHG in the atmosphere and potentially dramatic effects on climate change, but also on the acidification of the oceans: it seems as though the biodiversity of the seas is in danger as well. In fact, the problem of biodiversity is so serious that today 1000 times more species are currently becoming extinct than would be considered normal, and this rhythm of extinction is still increasing.

What causes even more concern (if that were possible) is the likely rise in sea levels worldwide, caused by an accelerated warming of the earth due to the release of methane gas $CH_4$ from the melting of the polar tundra (permafrost) and/or the melting of the ice cap in Greenland. Methane gas is a GHG with a $CO_2$-equivalent of 25 times!

The combined effects of climate change, declining biodiversity and exhaustion of our natural resources could ensure that mankind is the only species the earth has ever known that is capable of destroying all other species, and then itself. This is the conclusion of Richard Leakey,[77] one of the most prominent paleoanthropologists in the world, a professor of anthropology at Stony Brook University in New York and a former Kenyan politician:

> *"If you look back, the thing that strikes you, if you've got any sensitivity, is that extinction is the most common phenomena. Extinction is always driven by environmental change. Environmental change is always driven by climate change. Man accelerated, if not created, planet change phenomena; I think we have to recognize that the future is by no means a very rose one."*

As far as climate change is concerned, the challenge is not only to drastically re-duce our emissions of GHG, but to do so on a worldwide scale and in the limited time still available to us. Mathematical models, assessed by the *Intergovernmental Panel on Climate Change* (IPCC)[78] of the United Nations, are intended to persuade governments and peoples of the urgency of the situation. Their results make it possible to calculate the probability of future events that may result in significant collateral effects. In this context, the IPCC has evaluated a number of risk man-agement models, taking as a starting point the simplest form: *risk = impact x prob-ability*. Faced with an uncertain future (*e.g.* what is the *a priori* probability of any particular decision taking by political leaders on a world level?), combined with the need to make value judgements (*e.g.* what are acceptable and unacceptable risks?), scientists have found it difficult to satisfy even these modest requirements, since scientific methods are not appropriate for dealing with that kind of problem. Even so, the IPCC has attempted to estimate the probability that we will exceed certain thresholds for different emission scenarios, using *Bayesian statistics*.

The difficulty faced by scientists is that they cannot approach the problems in a scientific way. We *cannot deduct scientific experiments* or obtain *empirically based information about the future,* since we cannot perform or design experiments to col-lect data for things that have not yet happened. Consequently, quantitative models and forecasts of future events will continue to be statistical calculations, performed with stochastic variables, whose values are subject to variations due to chance. These values are represented by a probability distribution with a most likely value, its average, but with associated variances as a reminder of the uncertainty or our lack of information (or even ignorance) about the future. Furthermore, it is impera-tive to remember the implications of the findings of Thomas Bayes that *we must alter continuously our perception of the future based on newly available information previously unforeseeable that has become available once the future becomes the present.*

The Reverend Thomas Bayes FRS (1701-1761) was a rather conventional and un-talented 18th century Presbyterian minister. But he was a brilliant mathematician educated in logic. Bayes proved that by using all existing levels of knowledge, insights and theories, as well as all possible available data, we can calculate the *posterior probability* that an event will happen in the future. This is the so called Bayes' theorem. In its most simple form Bayes' theorem looks like:

$$P[A/B]=P[A].\frac{P[B/A]}{P[B]}$$

$P[A/B]$ is the *posterior* probability that an event $A$ – with a chance to occur expressed by its *prior* probability – will happen *and* will be caused by an event $B$ with a chance to occur of $P[B].P[A]$.

In other words the Bayes' theorem tells us that the chance or probability that an event will occur in the future results from two factors: (1) the chance that an event will occur in the present (*i.e.* prior probability $P[A]$) multiplied by (2) the chance it will occur in the future (*i.e. likelihood ratio* $P[B/A]/P[B]$). So posterior odds are proportional to the prior odds times the likelihood ratio. It is that simple!

The prior probability $P[A]$ is also called the *Base Rate* (*i.e.* de chance that something happens today measured by its prior probability). This means that the chance that anything will happen in the future remains very low if the *base rate* is very low! Only a huge increase in the likelihood ratio will change this. Understanding changes and fluctuations in the likelihood ratio are vital and utmost important in futures thinking. Understanding Bayer's theorem means also that with any new information we must revisit and reconsider our vison and beliefs about the future. Leaders confronted with VUCAT environments should particularly be sensitive to the implications of Bayes' theorem and change their opinion about future events when needed, but create as well a culture allowing open discussions, permitting to share all information and stimulating opinions to be expressed.

Actually Bayes believed his theorem was of no real use, simply because it had no practical application during his lifetime, primarily due to the lack of the necessary computer power. He died thinking that his contribution to science was minimal. We only know of his theorem because his friend, Richard Price FRS, published it in 1763, two years after Bayes' death (Bayes & Price, 1763). When the necessary computing power finally did become available, 250 years later, the enormous contribution of Bayes became evident. Today, the Bayes' theorem is at the heart of models relating to climate change, weather forecasting, astrophysics, social politics, economics and strategy. It also plays an increasingly important role in dealing with *big data*.

The *strategic conversation* about climate change exhibits all the characteristics of future thinking according to a Bayesian statistical approach. This is because in the long term – and the long term is always a turbulent environment – there is no certainty that climate change will occur in accordance with the forecasts of our mathematical models. It could be much worse than the models indicate or it could also be much better. Whatever policy is implemented today does not guarantee or remove the possibility that we still may be wrong. As Frank Knight said: "*There is no certainty about uncertainty*". The political debate on climate change might be closed, but the scientific debate is not. The scientific debate cannot be closed, simply because scientific method needs time to eliminate uncertainties by understanding causalities. Science progresses with history. For policy measures, however, time has already run out. If we do not act, and act soon, it will be too late. *Wicked problems* require decisions to be taken in situations of high complexity and high uncertainty. Such situations do not allow us the luxury of waiting until all relevant knowledge has been gathered.

The 21st century will also be the century in which we will need to rethink new forms of organization, in order to better stimulate and motivate people to work willingly. Research shows that people working in today's organizations only use half of their potential! It is worth looking at this in a broader perspective. Already in the 19th century but especially in the 20th century, efficiency improvements were at the centre of management sciences[79] and organizational development. This can easily be understood when comparing the number of people employed in agriculture today and 50 years ago. Who still works on Saturday morning? Who still works 45 hours a week? Let us take the Flanders region of Belgium as an example. In 1900, Flanders was so poor that workers were afraid to strike. The expression 'Poor Flanders', first used by August De Winne in 1904, still resonates in popular culture today. Even as late as the 1950s, Flanders was still relatively disadvantaged. Yet in less than 70 years, Flanders has become one of the richest regions in the world and is now in the world top in terms of labour productivity.[80]

The efficiency thinking that created this extraordinary increase in productivity and prosperity is primarily based on what is known as the *3S-principle*: simplification, standardization and specialization. This principle leads to centralization, as a result of which the *learning curve effect* and the directly related *experience curve effect* (*cf.* Bruce Henderson's Law), combined with *economies of scale,* lead to huge productivity and efficiency gains with consequently continuous cost reductions. Unfortunately, it was precisely this same centralization and automation that laid the basis for alienation between people, as well as between people and their craft. The division of tasks (simplification and standardization) also led to a division between those who *think* (leadership) and those who *do* (execution). The result was an under-utilisation of talents by those who execute, since most craftsmanship was replaced by automation, leaving either non-qualified jobs operating machines or qualified jobs for control and supervision. The end result was an over-strong centralization around a limited number of people who were allowed to decide and monitor everything, and the demotivation of almost everyone else, who felt as though they were not really needed, often combined with a growing dislike of organizations, companies, institutions and even political structures.

This under-utilisation of talent can still be found in many places today. But it is a challenge that is largely unseen and of which the importance is often under-estimated. But faced with global ageing, the growing importance of knowledge and creativity, increasing globalization and complexity, the necessary austerity measures caused by the 'Great Recession', and the need to maintain both our so-cial security system and our competitiveness, we are going to need – and use – all available talent.

This will require a thorough reflection on the way we organize our society in the years ahead. It will also require an in-depth political debate about how that society makes its decisions. We need urgently a *thinking futures debate*, since it is now patently clear that the current processes of political governance do not permit us to easily find solutions for the many future challenges we face.

In particular, the increase in complexity – driven by technology and globalization – means that our policy-making structures are becoming increasingly detached from the electoral base of the political leaders. This has resulted in a number of paradoxes, illustrating that we are in a transitional phase. For example, we expect that politicians elected locally, on the basis of local interests, will be able to solve global problems. This paradox leads to the repetitive organization of international conferences, which, notwithstanding perpetually high expectations and announced successes (*cf.* COP21 Paris Climate Change 2015), do not actually serve global public interests in the long term, but reflect instead the short-term selfish interests of individual nations, as was evident in both the Kyoto Protocol and the Rio+20 UN Conference.[81] Why do we continue to believe that we will ever be able to satisfactorily deal with global issues in this way?

To make matters worse, in many Western countries the fragmentation of political power has also slowed down the decision-making process in key areas where the challenges are crying out for strong and rapid public decisions. Are political lead-ers and journalists sufficiently aware of the seriousness of the problems facing us? Do they understand the insights, methods and approach that are necessary to find viable solutions? Might it not be better to create a powerful decision-making organization at a global level to deal with global problems of this kind?

Research into complexity also teaches us that *every complex problem has a simple and elegant solution that ... is acceptable to almost nobody*. This is because complex problems generally arise from important constraints and limitations imposed by the parties concerned. This means that choices are very difficult to make. These constraints (especially in socio-economic and geopolitical environments) are the result of expectations, demands, requirements or political visions. By imposing or accepting only a single vision, we can reduce every complexity and find a solution that is a perfect match for the wishes of a minority group but totally unacceptable to a majority, making the solution as a whole unusable. This is often the basis on which lobby groups, populists and pressure groups work.

If we were to apply this simplistic approach, then even the most complex problems – think, for example, of Belgian state reform[82], climate change, green mobility, nuclear energy, contentions planning issues, *etc.* – would have, according to some people, "very simple and easy solutions".

Our actions, thinking and structures still reflect this rigid rationality of the 3S-efficiency thinking of the past. True, this thinking (as previously mentioned) has led to an unprecedented increase in productivity and prosperity in Western countries in the 20th century. However, this was also accompanied by an unprecedented increase in the consumption of our natural resources. Paul Collier (2010) links future challenges in the field of raw materials management to the growing poverty in (Central) Africa:

> *"Restoring environmental order and eradicating global poverty*
> *have become the two defining challenges of our era ... As Nicholas*
> *Stern[83] argues, if we fail in either challenge, we fail in both."*

Collier concludes that one of the main reasons for the failure of the decision-making process so far is *egocentric rationality*. As long as people act from a self-centred vision about what they think needs to be done, the combined outcome will lead to conflict and undesirable results rather than agreement and beneficial change. The financial crisis of 2008 and the subsequent 'Great Recession' validate this argument: no one pleaded guilty, everyone acted egocentrically and did what was 'acceptable' and 'justified' from the perspective of their own limited rationality. However, the combined result of their actions was the most severe social and economic crisis since the end of the Second World War, still labelled today by some as the 'Contained Depression'[84] in comparison to the 'Great Depression' of the 1930s. Its dramatic effects in Europe – including the threat to the existence of the euro as the currency of the Eurozone and even to the wider stability of the European Union as a whole – only became visible to their full extent in the period 2011 to 2015. Yet strange at it may seem in the face of such a severe warning, the initial signals suggest that the banking eco-system has learned very little from this crisis (*cf.* debates about corporate governance and bonuses, speculation, risk and ethical behaviour). As a result, very few fundamental changes have been made to avoid a future repetition of the 2008 catastrophe. Regulatory amendments have also been minimal. In short, everyone is returning to the old habits of the past.

Social systems are very hard to change and new ones take a lot of learning. This same 'I'-oriented behaviour is also at the heart of the ecological crisis that threatens to destroy a multitude of species – including our own human culture – by the end of this century (*cf.* Martin Rees). As in so many other areas, we are again misjudging the speed at which fundamental changes can happen and will occur.

Richard Nisbett believes that this egocentric behaviour is strongly embedded in Western culture and leads to what he calls the *fundamental attribution error* or the failure to recognize that situational forces may explain our behaviour and hence the different evolutions towards possible futures.

This is not a plea for a romantic return to nature, nor is it a reason to think that technology in due course will perhaps not find the solutions we need. It is, however, a plea for methods that will allow us all to deal with complex and wicked problems by looking at all their possible dimensions. Economic growth is just one of these dimensions. Solving the challenges of the future will oblige us to define our wealth in terms of multiple dimensions.

Hopefully, this very brief overview of the future challenges facing our world will illustrate that perhaps other forms of thinking about the future are needed. The existing methods, structures and institutions are not wholly suited to deal with these challenges. We need to realize this before it is too late.

## A need for different methods for future thinking

At the invitation of the Oxford Martin School, Al Gore, 45th Vice-President of the U.S., gave a lecture at the *Examination School* of the University of Oxford on 31 October 2013.

As a remarkably gifted speaker, he captivates and fascinates his audience from start to finish, even though he is discussing some very profound and thoughtful topics, based on his book *The Future* (Gore, 2013). His analysis and views on future challenges are very similar to the insights, analysis and conclusions reached in recent years by international policy think-tanks like the *Oxford Martin School* in Oxford, *Bruegel* or the *European Policy Centre* (EPC) in Brussels, the *Hudson Institute* in New York or *Futuribles* in Paris. These are also the same challenges discussed during the meetings of the *Global Agenda Councils* (GAC) or the *Global Strategic Foresight Community* (GSFC) of the World Economic Forum (WEF), which we have summarized briefly in this chapter.

**Al Gore (l) – Derrick Gosselin (r).**
**31 October 2013, Examination School, University of Oxford.**
ord.

*© 2013 Oxford Martin School.*

Apparently, more and more key decision-makers with important responsibilities are beginning to understand the exceptionally *wicked* nature of the problems we face, for which solutions in the coming decades urgently need to be found. However, few of them realize that there is also a need to develop innovative approaches and methodologies to meet these wicked challenges. Perhaps they do not yet fully appreciate that finding solutions to wicked problems also encompasses an understanding of the available *range of methods* and associated ways of thinking that we have at our disposal to address these problems. The following quotation from Alfred Einstein dating back to 1948 expresses precisely this point. His wicked problem was trying to survive the atomic age, but his words are equally applicable to the challenges of today:

> *"Our situation is not comparable to anything in the past. It is impossible, therefore, to apply methods and measures which at an earlier age might have been sufficient. We must revolutionize our thinking, revolutionize our actions, and must have the courage to revolutionize relations among nations of the world. Clichés of yesterday will no longer do today, and will, no doubt, be hopelessly out of date tomorrow."*[85]

So what exactly do we know about this relationship between *problem, method and solution?*

In 2002, Daniel Kahneman was awarded the Nobel Prize in Economics[86] for his discoveries, made together with Amos Tversky (1937-1996), about how people make judgements and decisions in uncertain conditions (Kahneman, 2011). More particularly, their research investigated systematic cognitive biases or judgment errors in human decision-making and risk handling (*cf.* heuristics and biases theory). His Nobel Prize is even more remarkable, since Kahneman is not an economist but a psychologist! His most famous (but certainly not his only) contribution to economics is the *prospect theory*,[87] again developed with Tversky. In this theory they showed that our *prospect* of losing something affects us negatively (*i.e.* makes us miserable) *twice as much* as gaining the same thing affects us positively (*i.e.* makes us happy).

Other research by Kahneman also gave new insights into the *problem-method-solution* relationship. He discovered that *"the capabilities needed to understand, correctly evaluate and solve complex problems are precisely the same capabilities needed to be able to assess and recognize the qualities and competences of the people that present to us the potential solutions to these problems."*

This means that in order to evaluate and assess employees and close advisors, leaders actually use the same skills as when they try to understand and solve complex problems. Consequently, leaders who are not capable of correctly assessing or understanding all aspects of complex problems are also not capable of correctly evaluating and assessing the advice of their direct reports, close advisors or consultants! Because of this, they accept the wrong opinions, choose the wrong options and deal with the problems badly.

The problems we are facing are so complex that mediocre leaders are not able to resolve them by themselves. Unfortunately, they also prevent people with the necessary knowledge and skills from being heard or from addressing the problems in an innovative and adequate way! As a rule, mediocre leaders usually replace competent people with second-rate individuals they understand and who share their own views.

This leads to a completely mediocre organization, where mediocre people supplant good people at all levels. As soon as an organization – any organization – needs to deal with complex problems, it is essential to appoint the best possible leaders to senior management positions. Keeping incompetent leaders in top jobs to handle complex situations imposed by the environment will eventually create myopic organizations that will be repeatedly shocked and surprised by 'unforeseen' events.

**Lord Martin Rees (l) – Derrick Gosselin (r).**
**23 February 2009. Divinity School, University of Oxford.**

© *2009 Photographer: Yves Fassin.*

So what is the best way to tackle the challenges of the future adequately? We posed this question to the world-renowned Professor Martin John Rees OM FRS (Lord Rees of Ludlow), former President of the Royal Society[88], while attending a lecture given by him on 23 February 2009 at the *Sheldonian Theatre* in Oxford about the insights he expressed in his book *The Final Century* (Rees 2003). His answer must be framed within the context of the trends and challenges previously described in this chapter. Taking into account his research background, we expected Martin Rees to reply that all available financial and human resources should be urgently allocated to innovation. Not so. In fact, his response was surprising:

> *"We must first and foremost motivate brilliant young people to study political sciences. We must convince them to effectively go into the political arena. Moreover, it is also paramount that they commit themselves to academic research in order to find new international political decision-making systems that will make it possible to build structures to address global problems. We need more political innovation and political R&D!"*

We couldn't agree more. But how do you discover these new and innovative political decision-making methods? We believe a new approach to problem solving is mandatory and that such a new approach will require more multidisciplinary research. Perhaps even a new academic discipline that assembles scholars from different fields of expertise like law, diplomacy, political sciences, geopolitical and defence sciences, organizational behaviour, psychology, technology and engineering sciences, and management sciences. Strategic foresight and *futures* thinking for political decision-making will inevitably occupy a prominent place within this new discipline. The first tentative steps in the right direction have already been taken, but the new discipline still needs to be established and developed at many more universities in many more countries, including in Belgium. Having said that, it is possible that universities are no longer the best place – at least not exclusively – to develop these new approaches. An important role can also be played by international think-tanks, government agencies and academies. Independence, neutrality, credibility and access to political decision-makers are essential key success factors – and therefore part of the solution to wicked problems.

The OECD, the G20 and the governments of many developing economies, joined by an increasing number of companies and non-profit organizations, are taking more and more *thinking futures*-based initiatives, as well as creating institutions to foster those initiatives. The aim is not only to generate a *futures*-based vision, but also to crystallize policy choices, which is crucial for the survival and development of any organization! Without a clear vision of the future, resources become fragmented, there is no adequate agenda, no focus in policy and confusion in decision-making on such vital matters as investment choice and competence build-up. This jeopardizes the future of the organization as a learning organization. Furthermore, it becomes difficult to evaluate opportunities, so that scarce resources are badly deployed. Without future thinking, every shock will be a surprise. And in today's world, shocks seem to follow each other faster than ever before.

Developing a vision based on futures thinking is similar to proposing a hypothesis that constantly needs to be challenged, reviewed and adapted in response to the rapid and unexpected changes imposed by a dynamic and complex environment. Without *futures* thinking, without a vision, we will always be too late. Thinking about futures prepares us for uncertainty, for what we may not expect. Pragmatic problem solving (*i.e.* dealing with the problem when it occurs) yields very few (if any) positive results; worse, it is most likely to lead to catastrophic outcomes when confronted with wicked problems. The reasons are obvious: surprise means lack of preparation; lack of preparation means loss of time; loss of time means more complexity; more complexity means fewer options. In the end, the environment will impose the remaining options on you. All you have done is increase the turbulence!

## Futures initiatives throughout the world

Fortunately, there are nowadays many worldwide initiatives to assist in the development of long-term visions to support governments, businesses and society. Undeniably, the 'Great Recession' has accelerated this evolution, even if by mid-2015 the stock markets have recovered to the pre-recession levels of 2007. Here is a selection of the most important of these initiatives.

## Table 7: Futures Institutes Worldwide[89]

| Country | Name | Description | Internet |
|---|---|---|---|
| Austria | The International Institute for Applied Systems Analysis | Conducts interdisciplinary studies on environmental, economic, technological and social issues in the context of the human dimensions of global change. | www.iiasa.ac.at |
| Australia | Foresight International | Focuses on creating theory and practice of social foresight. | www.foresightinternational.com.au |
| Azerbaijan | The Azerbaijan Future Studies Society | Established in 2006 as a non-profit research centre. It is the first futures studies centre in Azerbaijan. | www.futurestudies.az |
| China | | Research within the Chinese Academy of Social Sciences. | http://casseng.cssn.cn |
| Denmark | Copenhagen Institute for Futures Studies | Decision-making in public and private organizations by creating awareness of the future. | www.cifs.dk/en |
| Estonia | The Estonian Institute for Futures Studies | Contributes to the development of the Estonian Society. | www.eti.ee |
| EU | The European Foresight Monitoring Network | Monitors ongoing and emerging foresight activities and disseminates information about these activities to a network of policy researchers and foresight practitioners. | http://ec.europa.eu/research/foresight/10/article_3962_en.htm |
| | The Institute for Prospective Technological Studies | Provides support to the EU policy-making process by developing science-based responses to policy challenges that have both a socio-economic as well as a scientific/technological dimension. | https://ec.europa.eu/jrc/en/institutes/ipts |
| | The European Political Strategy Centre | Created in 2015, it provides future policy advice to the President of the European Commission. | http://ec.europa.eu/epsc |
| Finland | Finland Futures Research Centre | The only academic futures research organization in Finland and the biggest in the Nordic countries. | www.utu.fi/en/units/ffrc |
| France | Futuribles | Centre for prospective studies and foresight. Futuribles explores current issues, possible futures, policies and strategies. | www.futuribles.fr |

| Country | Name | Description | Internet |
|---|---|---|---|
| France | France Stratégie | Created in 2013, it advises the government on important future issues. Successor of the Central Planning Office. | www.strategie.gouv.fr |
| Germany | The Institute for Futures Studies and Technology Assessment | A non-profit research institute. Its main tasks are the realization of research projects, delivering expert opinions, and advising political and industrial decision-makers. | www.izt.de/en |
| Global | The World Future Council | Brings the interests of future generations to the centre of policy-making. The Council addresses challenges to our common future and provides decision-makers with effective policy solutions. | www.worldfuturecouncil.org |
| | OECD<br><br>International Futures Programme | Provides the organization with an early warning of emerging issues, pinpoints major developments, and analyses key long-term concerns to help governments map strategy. | www.oecd.org/futures |
| | World Economic Forum<br><br>Global Strategic Foresight Community | The purpose is to provide a peer network to compare and contrast insights, as well as to positively shape future-related industry, regional and global agendas. | http://reports.weforum.org/global-strategic-foresight-community |
| Israel | The Interdisciplinary Centre for Technological Analysis & Forecasting | Is a research centre specializing in technology forecasting, foresight, assessment, and long-term planning. | http://ictaf.tau.ac.il/index.asp?lang=eng |
| Netherlands | Scientific Council for Government Policy (WRR) | An independent advisory body to the government on important future issues. | www.wrr.nl/en |
| Singapore | Centre for Strategic Futures | Positions the Singapore government to navigate emerging strategic challenges and harness potential opportunities by building capacities, mind-sets, expertise and tools for strategic anticipation and risk management; developing insights into future trends, discontinuities and strategic surprises; and communicating insights to decision-makers for informed policy planning. | www.csf.gov.sg |

| Country | Name | Description | Internet |
|---------|------|-------------|----------|
| Sweden | Royal Swedish Academy of Engineering Sciences | Technology and problems in society. | www.iva.se/iva-in-english |
| | Institute for Future Studies | An independent research foundation. The focus is to promote a future-oriented perspective in Swedish research, and to use and develop appropriate theories and methods. The Institute promotes open and broad discussion about possibilities and threats to future social development. | www.iffs.se/en |
| | Swedish Foundation for Strategic Research | Research in natural science, engineering and medicine. | www.stratresearch.se/en |
| South Africa | The Institute for Futures Research | A research institution specializing in futures studies, primarily as a support service for knowledge and strategic management. | www.ifr.sun.ac.za |
| U.K. | The Foresight Programme and Horizon Scanning Centre | Provides visions of the future using robust science to be used by policy-makers to inform government policy and strategy, and to improve how science and technology are used within government and by society. | www.foresight.gov.uk |
| | Oxford Martin School | A world-leading centre at the University of Oxford, pioneering research, debate and policy for a sustainable and inclusive future. | www.oxfordmartin.ox.ac.uk |
| | The Future of Humanity Institute | A multidisciplinary research institute at the University of Oxford. | www.fhi.ox.ac.uk |
| U.S.A. | Institute for the Future | An independent, non-profit research group, created in 1968 as a spring-off of RAND. Focuses on the identification of emerging trends and discontinuities that will transform global society and the global marketplace. | www.iftf.org |
| | Hawaii Research Center for Futures Studies | Institution for futures research, consulting and education. | www.futures.hawaii.edu |
| | World Future Society | A non-profit, scientific and educational association of people interested in how social and technological developments are shaping the future. | www.wfs.org |

| Country | Name | Description | Internet |
|---------|------|-------------|----------|
| U.S.A. | The Millennium Project | A global participatory futures research think-tank of futurists, scholars, business planners and policy-makers who work for international organizations, governments, corporations, NGOs, and universities. | www.millennium-project.org |
| | The World Futures Studies Federation | A global network of practicing futurists, researchers, teachers, scholars, policy analysts, activists, and others from over 60 countries. Its mission is to promote futures education and research. | www.wfsf.org |
| | The Center for Millennial Development | The Center for Millennial Development at Boston University is the world's largest academic research centre dedicated to millennial studies. | www.mille.org |
| | International Institute of Forecasters | Dedicated to developing and furthering the generation, distribution and use of knowledge on forecasting. | http://forecasters.org |
| | RAND Corporation | A research organization that develops solutions to public policy challenges, to help make communities throughout the world safer and more secure, healthier and more prosperous. | www.rand.org |
| | Hudson Institute | Founded in 1961 by Herman Kahn, the Hudson Institute challenges conventional thinking and helps manage strategic transitions to the future through interdisciplinary studies. | www.hudson.org |

We will now look closer at some of the more prominent initiatives highlighted in Table 7, without any ambition of being exhaustive:

- OECD: International Futures Programme.
- The European Union: Institute of Prospective Technology Studies – The European Political Strategy Centre.
- The United Kingdom: Foresight Programme.
- France: *France Stratégie: commissariat général à la stratégie et à la prospective.*
- Netherlands: Scientific Council for Government Policy.
- Sweden: Institute for Future Studies.
- Singapore: Risk Assessment and Horizon Scanning.
- The University of Oxford: Oxford Future Forum – Oxford Martin School – Institute for Science, Innovation and Technology – Smith School of Enterprise and the Environment.
- World Economic Forum: Global Strategic Foresight Community.

## The OECD initiatives

The *Organization for Economic Cooperation and Development* (OECD) is an offshoot of the famous plan to rebuild Europe after the Second World War. This plan was suggested during the 'Marshall Plan'[90] speech on 5 June 1947 at the University of Harvard by the U.S. Secretary of State Georges Catlett Marshall, Jr. (1880-1959), former U.S. Army Chief of Staff during the Second World War and a future Noble Peace Prize laureate.

Launched in 1948, the *Marshall Plan* – officially the European Recovery Programme – was actually an organization formed to supervise both the food distribution and the economic recovery of Europe. By 1961, its role and mission had changed and the OECD in its current form was created. The organization is located in the beautiful *Château de la Muette* in Paris. Today, the OECD is an international economic organization formed by the governments of 34 industrialized and majorly developed countries that are committed to democracy and the free market-driven economy. The OECD's executive committee meets in the Roger Ockrent (1914-1974) Room, named after the Belgian diplomat who was the first chairman of the executive committee from 1961 until 1974.

The OECD offers a forum for governments to study and formulate the best possible social and economic policies. This includes benchmarking the results of their policies, comparing and exchanging policy experiences, seeking answers to common problems, and sharing and identifying good practices. They also coordinate domestic and international economic policies between the participating countries.

The OECD also promotes the *International Futures Programme* (IFP). The IFP has been providing strategic, long-term thinking and horizon scanning since 1990. IFP events offer a platform where policy-makers can freely confront their visions and concerns about the future, seek the views of others and engage in a stimulating dialogue. In this way, they gain a better understanding of the issues at stake. A variety of tools is used, ranging from horizon scanning and trend analysis to scenario construction, focus groups and policy analysis. In particular, the IFP works on the rapid identification of new trends and unexpected emerging events. It also develops new topics and provides challenging perspectives for strategic conversations sometimes not considered by other OECD departments.

It is noteworthy that the IFP reports directly to the Secretary-General. In this way, the Secretary-General not only has an instrument available to explore long-term issues, but above all has an instrument to deal with unexpected problems at the level of the global economy.

The IFP is often co-financed by donations and contributions from governments, research institutes, companies and foundations.

Recent publications give a picture of this fresh approach but also highlight the topics selected and addressed for futures research since 2007. These topics can be grouped by technology, economy, government and society:

- Space Economy at a Glance (2014).
- The Future of the Ocean Economy (2014).
- Strategic Transport Infrastructure Needs to 2030 (2012).
- The Future of Families to 2030 (2011).
- Future Global Shocks: Improving Risk Governance (2011).
- The *Bioeconomy* to 2030 (2009).
- Space technology and climate change: implications for water management, marine resources and maritime transport (2008).
- Infrastructure to 2030: a policy plan for electricity, water and transport (2007).

## The European Union: the Institute for Prospective Technology Studies & the European Political Strategy Centre

The *Institute for Prospective Technological Studies* (IPTS) is one of the seven scientific institutes of the Joint Research Centres (JRC) of the European Commission. Approximately 200 employees of the IPTS are housed in the State-of-the-Art Expo building in the *Isla de la Cartuja*, one of the technology parks in the Spanish city of Seville.

Since 1994, the IPTS promotes a better understanding of the relationship between technology, economy and society. Its mission is to provide E.U. policy-makers with independent, evidence-based scientific and technical support in the fields of socio-economics, science and technology, under the generic name 'techno-economic research'. The IPTS works mainly at the request of the Directorates-General of the European Commission to help solve key social challenges, but recently there were also assignments for the European Parliament.

The IPTS makes use of multidisciplinary teams that also use *foresight* methods. Its competence lies in the analysis of policy options and the assessment of the impact of policy. The IPTS makes socio-economic analyses of new technologies. It is particularly noteworthy that the IPTS uses the *foresight* method to build consensus between many stakeholders and policy-makers for highly complex techno-economic issues. Current reports and research projects cover techno-economic futures thinking in the fields of sustainable development, smart specialization, industrial and clean technology, energy, transport, agriculture and rural development, and the information society.

Alongside the IPTS, the European Commission has also created the European Political Strategy Centre.

The *European Political Strategy Centre* (EPSC) delivers future oriented policy advice to the President of the European Commission. One of its important projects is the *European Strategy and Policy Analysis System* (ESPAS). The aim of ESPAS is to identify the main global trends with a time horizon of 2030, assess the implications of these trends for the E.U., and review the challenges and policy options facing decision-makers.

ESPAS produced its first major report in 2015: *Global Trends to 2030*.[91] This report draws on several years of work and identifies key questions for policy-makers to address in the coming years. It covers issues as diverse as the reshaping of the international economy, the rise of 'people power', the impact of a growing global middle class, increasing inequality, power shifts in international relations and the nature and extent of climate change.

## The United Kingdom: Foresight Programme

In May 1993, William Waldegrave (Lord Waldegrave of North Hill), British Minister for Science, launched a white book entitled *Realizing Our Potential: A Strategy for Science, Engineering and Technology*. This white book was a brilliant piece of good government practice. It recommended – and rightly so – that the British Government should establish a department for technological future planning to be led by a *Chief Scientific Advisor*, reporting directly to the Prime Minister.

The newly established department was located at 1, Victoria Street, London – not far from the Houses of Parliament and close to the centre of government and political life. The intention was clear: to ensure a close interaction among scientists, industrialists, ministers, government officials and public servants, through identifying future opportunities and threats, especially in the field of science, engineering and technology.

In 1994, the first foresight round started. Experts from industry, government and the academic world were brought together in 15 panels. Each panel investigated opportunities in certain domains. They looked at emerging markets and technological opportunities for the next 20 years. Out if this, priorities and a provisional action plan were drawn up to exploit them. More than 10 000 people were surveyed. In 1995, this led to a final action plan encompassing approximately 360 recommendations. In each domain, the report identified the likely social, economic and market trends for the next 10 to 20 years.

In April 1999, the second round started. Three thematic and ten sector panels each looked at a specific area of the economy.

In this way, the limited technological focus from the first round was broadened with a quest for opportunities that could arise from the interaction of innovations in science and technology with wider social and market trends. Each panel also looked at the implications of education and analysed the skills and training that would be required for the future and for sustainable development. They further looked at the future of a specific domain in order to identify all opportunities and threats with which the country might conceivably be faced during the next 10 to 20 years and even beyond. The report was published in 2000.

In that same year 2000, the then Minister of Science and Innovation David Sainsbury FRS (Lord Sainsbury of Turville) also announced a revision of the *Foresight* programme. His intention was to build on the success of the first two rounds, but with even more focus on opportunities. This review concluded that the programme needed to focus more on science and technology projects and that more flexibility was needed for burgeoning and unexpected developments. It was precisely in that area that extra value could be created. To increase the flexibility, panels that kept their agenda static for a long time were abandoned in favour of panels with a dynamic calendar that could be customized faster. There are now two starting points to generate science and technology projects: they are either related to problems for which science has an (almost) ready-made solution or related to domains that look at new applications and technologies that have not yet been clearly defined. These foresight projects typically take 24 months to complete.

In 2015, after more than 20 years of outstanding work, Victoria Street still retains its original mission of promoting and structuring futures thinking and stimulating interdisciplinary interaction, as expressed by William Waldegrave in 1993. In the meantime, the *Government Office for Science* (GOS) has been created as a government agency and is now responsible for foresight and futures thinking, as well as advising the U.K. Government on policy and decision-making grounded in robust scientific evidence and long-term thinking. The GOS is led by the *Government Chief Scientific Adviser* (GCSA) (*cf.* Sir David King FRS, Sir Mark Walport FRS). Its offices are also located at 1, Victoria Street, in the same building as the *Department for Business, Innovation & Skills*. Particularly noteworthy are the direct and dual reporting lines of the GCSA to both the Prime Minister and to members of Cabinet. The GCSA also co-chairs the Prime Minister's *Council for Science and Technology*.

The Government Office for Science is in charge of three types of projects and programmes. They relate to policy futures, foresight and horizon scanning. *Policy futures projects* are short, often only 6 to 12 month studies that provide futures and evidence analysis to fill a specific gap in current policy understanding. *Foresight projects* are more in-depth studies of roughly 24 months duration that build a comprehensive evidence base on major issues looking 20 to 80 years into the future. *Horizon scanning projects* are studies looking at discrete issues 10 to 15 years in the future.

Examples of selected topics for policy futures (P), foresight (F) and horizon scanning (HS) projects[92] over the period 2006-2015 are listed below. This gives an overview of the different *futures agenda(s)* of the U.K. Government, illustrating the issues that can plausibly be expected to have an important impact on society in the years ahead:

- Future of cities (P)(2015)
- Future of aging (P)(2014)
- Future of manufacturing (F)(2013)
- Technology and innovation futures: UK growth opportunities for the 2020s (HS)(2012)
- Future of food and farming (F)(2011)
- Migration and global environmental change: future challenges and opportunities (F)(2011)
- International dimensions of climate warming (F)(2011)
- Mental capital and wellbeing (F)(2008)
- Sustainable energy management: the role of science and technology (HS) (2007)
- Reducing obesity: future choices (F)(2007)
- Infectious diseases: preparing for the future (F)(2006)
- Intelligent infrastructure futures (F)(2006)

In January 2013, the U.K. Government created a new *Cabinet Secretary's Advisory Group*, composed of a group of senior civil servants and chaired by the Cabinet Secretary. This newly formed group leads and coordinates all existing horizon scanning projects within government and commissions new strands of work to inform major areas of policy. Although considerable horizon scanning work was already being done in government departments and in the GOS, it was decided that efforts could be better coordinated to improve efficiency and ensure greater capability in understanding and addressing relevant issues, given the increasingly turbulent environment.

The cross-government Horizon Scanning Programme aims to embed better horizon scanning capabilities in the policy-making process in the U.K. Civil Service and to coordinate activity. The Horizon Scanning Programme must also ensure that implications for policy are highlighted at the right levels; that a common baseline of understanding is established across government departments and organizations; and that best practice is shared. The Cabinet Secretary, through the Cabinet Secretary's Advisory Group, leads the programme. They are the ultimate customer for the existing network of officials in various government departments and agencies whose task is to escalate emergent trends and issues. They also coordinate work on cross-cutting themes that will affect more than one part of government. A small *Horizon Scanning Secretariat* within the Cabinet Office's Government Innovation Group, working closely with the *Foresight Horizon Scanning Centre* in the Government Office for Science (GOS), supports the Cabinet Secretary's Advisory Group.

Three ministers provide ministerial oversight for the programme: the Minister for the Cabinet Office, the Minister for Government Policy and the Minister of State for the Cabinet Office. They are informed of the findings, conclusions and any policy recommendations arising from meetings of the Cabinet Secretary's Advisory Group. They also meet periodically to review the programme and to commission further future work where required.

The Horizon Scanning Programme has focused since 2013 on the following areas: emerging technologies, emerging economies, the changing supply and demand of resources, the changing social attitudes of young people and the future of demographic change in the U.K. An excellent report resulting from this approach is the *Strategic Trends Programme: Global Strategic Trends – Out to 2045*, [93] published by the Ministry of Defence in 2014.

## France Stratégie: commissariat général à la stratégie et à la prospective

*France Stratégie* was established in 2013. Its origins go back to the *Commissariat Général du Plan* (CGP) established in 1946 by General Charles de Gaulle (1890-1970) in response to a proposal from Jean Monnet (1888-1979), who became its first commissioner. The CGP played a significant role in the reconstruction of the French economy in the post-war period.

The CGP existed from 1946 until 2006, when it was reformed into the *Centre d'Analyse Stratégique* (CAS), before finally becoming (by a decree of 22 April 2013) the *Commissariat général à la stratégie et à la prospective* (General Commission for Strategy and Foresight), more generally known as *France Stratégie*.

Its current mission is to provide strategic advice to the executive office of France. In order to fulfil their mission, they focus on four key actions:

- *Evaluating* public policies independently.
- *Anticipating changes* in the economy, society, sustainable development and technology; analysing the associated issues these topics raise in the medium term; preparing for political decision.
- *Debating* through the organization of open strategic conversations, discussions or dialogues with social partners, civil society and business, as well as the community of experts and academia.
- *Proposing policies / reforms / guidance* to government, highlighting the possible trade-offs, foreign experiences and the respective positions of the actors.

*France Stratégie* is also responsible for coordinating a network of eight advisory bodies: (1) *Economic Analysis Council*, (2) *Pensions Policy Board*, (3) *Employment Policy Board*, (4) *High Council for the Family*, (5) *High Council for the Future of Health Insurance*, (6) *High Council for the Financing of Social Protection*, (7) *National Council for the Industry*, (8) *Centre for Future Studies and International Information*.

As such, *France stratégie* is able to counsel or to assist the Prime Minister and the President of France on questions related to futures thinking and *sensemaking*, as well as supporting policy decisions, organizing public consultations and evaluating policies.

## The Netherlands: Scientific Council for Government Policy

The Scientific Council for Government Policy[94] (WRR) is an independent advisory body for the Dutch Government, created in 1976. Its task is to offer scientific-based advice to government concerning future trends, developments or issues that are of great importance for society. The recommendations support the future-oriented direction of government policy. The Dutch Government can use this advice in three ways: to adjust existing policies; to develop new policies; or to support decision-making processes.

The WRR also seeks to stimulate the scientific debate. Based on international scientific literature and knowledge, all assumptions are questioned, possible alternative policies are analysed and solutions are presented with an eye for future developments. The WRR therefore forms a bridge between scientific expertise and policy. The council has more than 30 years of experience and has managed to find the right balance between scientific independence in determining future problems and political credibility in order to translate this advice into policy. A selection of the projects the WRR will focus on in coming years includes:

- Big data, privacy and security
- The future of work
- Security and defence policy
- Super diversity
- Public tasks within the E.U.
- Philanthropy

## Sweden: Institute for Futures Studies (IFFS)

In 1971, a government commission was set up in Sweden to investigate what form futures studies should take. It was led by cabinet minister and subsequent Noble Peace Prize laureate Alva Myrdal (1902-1986). The commission's final report was entitled *Choosing One's Future*. The government followed its recommendation and in 1973 the *Secretariat for Futures Studies* was founded, directly accountable to the Prime Minister's Office. In 1987, the government decided to transform the Secretariat into an independent institution, at which point the *Institute for Futures Studies* was established. Today, the Institute is an independent research foundation financed partly through a government subsidy and partly through external funding from research councils. Its board members are still appointed by the government.

The IFFS task is to promote a future-oriented perspective in Swedish research; to use and develop appropriate futures theories and methods; and to promote open and broad discussion about possibilities and threats to future social development. In addition to its research activities, the Institute organizes seminars and workshops, some of which are oriented towards the public at large.

The IFFS works in close cooperation with the *Royal Swedish Academy of Engineering Sciences* (Table 7), which was founded in 1919 and was the first engineering science academy in the world. The Academy has a longstanding tradition of clarifying the potential of technology and problems in society, the economic consequences of new technology and prerequisites for sustainable development.

The main topic selected for the 2015-2020 research programme is *Social Change in the 21ˢᵗ Century*. This programme will focus on large-scale social change and its implications for both the present and the future. The use of advanced simulation methods and large-scale databases are at the core of the programme. Particular attention will be given to:

- Changes in social and political values
- The economic impact of demographic change
- Social segregation processes
- Methods useful for analysing and predicting long-term change

## Singapore: Risk Assessment and Horizon Scanning

Singapore is today, along with the Scandinavian countries, perhaps the ultimate example of a nation whose policy is oriented by future thinking. The Government of Singapore has been investing strongly in future thinking for many years and currently has the most advanced systems of future thinking in the world.

Singapore began its future planning efforts as an experiment in its Ministry of Defence in the late 1980s. In 1995, the Government set up the *Scenario Planning Office* in the Prime Minister's Office to develop scenarios from a whole-of-government perspective. The office was renamed the *Strategic Policy Office* in 2003 to reflect the strengthened links between foresight work and strategy formulation.

Every few years, an exercise in scenario planning is organised on a national level. The scenarios that are conceived serve as a basis for the strategic planning process of the individual ministries. The Government uses the scenario method in addition to the annual cycle of strategic planning and also for the annual budgetary cycle.

The Singapore Government goes beyond the formatting of studies and the organization of scenario projects. It also implements a process with regular strategic conversations. Through a series of workshops and discussion forums, the leading figures in the public sector are involved and a consensus is built around a complete strategic agenda. Singaporean officials now almost instinctively ask themselves *'what if?'* questions about the problems they face. In this way, all public services have a common frame of reference about the future and all the different planning units of the ministries speak the same language and share the same concepts of scenario planning.

This is not a coincidence. Research shows that scenarios do indeed help to create a common language, while a common language in turn creates a common reality (*cf.* Wittgenstein). Much about the role of language in organizations is still unknown. We do know, however, that in the few companies where research has been carried out it has already been established that a common and well-understood word usage (*i.e.* the same words meaning the same concepts for everyone) accelerates the decision-making process.

In 2004, in addition to the scenario method, a second programme was launched: *Risk Assessment and Horizon Scanning* (RAHS). The objective was to build competence in the research of complex cases in which cause and effect are difficult to distinguish. For this, a series of complementary methods is used. Special software was even developed to assist analysts in the detection and investigation of emerging strategic threats and opportunities over a period of two to five years. This software created a common platform for all relevant administrations and agencies, allowing all the analysts to collaborate effectively for research purposes and for the creation of a common perspective. They are encouraged to collectively build new models for their policy domain and to keep them up to date. They actively review each other's work and question the assumptions on which that work is based. Originally, the RAHS programme was set up for security services; today, it is used for a wide range of projects, for a multitude of agencies, and for projects where cooperation between different services is important.

Recently, there was a new initiative, designed to further integrate risk management into the complete strategic planning framework of the Government. This project is still running, but the goal is clearly defined: the intention is not only to map out the specific operational risks for each ministry, but also to monitor the wider strategic risks that can affect Singapore as a nation.

All these initiatives are complementary and reinforce each other. Both the programme scenario and the RAHS project offer a range of methods from which the analyst can choose to tackle his or her specific problem. The RAHS project provides techniques for domain-specific problems, where software can help when things get very complex. Risk management integrates the analyses from the scenario planning and from the RAHS projects to design strategies that help to decrease the impact of unexpected events.

The Singapore Government continues to build on its capacity for future thinking. Recently, yet another new initiative was introduced under the working name *Scenario Planning Plus*. The aim is to make each element of the already successful policy-oriented methods even more effective. In particular, it is intended to further strengthen the three building blocks of the process:

- Maintaining the strength of the scenario method
- Incorporating new techniques
- Strengthening the coordination of the platforms for strategic conversations and policy development

To make sure that this project has everything it needs to succeed, in 2009 the Singaporean Government created a new institution: the *Centre for Strategic Futures* (CSF) (Table 7). This illustrates the commitment of the public services to continue to develop and enhance the country's competence in the field of future thinking. The aim of the centre is to promote an overall government approach, based on scenario planning, towards thinking about the strategic challenges of today and tomorrow. The CSF meets over 200 thought leaders each year through incoming visits, overseas trips, paid consultancies, interviews and curated events. It also meets regularly with futurists from various sections of the Singapore Government to share best practices and to build up the practice of foresight within government. Topics on the 2011-2014 strategic agenda were:

- The evolving role of the state
- Using causal layered analysis to explore the socio-economic aspirations of Singaporeans
- Turning risks into opportunities
- From foresight to strategy: emerging strategic issues 2.0
- Capacity building – developing talent in futures
- Humanity 2.0
- The future of work
- Futures conversations
- Global-Asia confluence

- Governing for the future: what governments can do
- Emerging strategic issues project 2.0
- Mapping and navigating a volatile, complex risk environment through networked national risk management.

## The University of Oxford

The University of Oxford has a long tradition of coordinating interdisciplinary scientific research on futures thinking. The establishment of the *Oxford Martin School*[95] (OMS), founded by James Martin in 2005, reinforced the university's leading role in foresight practise.

Dr James Martin (1933-2013) graduated from Keble College, Oxford to become a prominent ICT technology visionary and prolific author. Martin endowed what became the Oxford Martin School with $150 million. By virtue of this remarkable endowment, Martin became the single biggest private donor to Oxford University in its 900-year history, more generous even than Sir Thomas Bodley, the diplomat, scholar and founder in 1598 of the *Bodleian Library*. In fact, Martin's benefaction is the largest single gift to any university in Britain. Martin asked Professor Ian Goldin, previously at the World Bank and a former adviser to the South African President Nelson Mandela, to become its first director, from 2007 until 2016.

Martin founded his school in the belief that this century, and more specifically the period 2005-2040, will be a crucial turning point for the human race. The sheer speed of change means that mankind now has the power to destroy countless possibilities for future generations, but equally has the potential to dramatically improve the wellbeing of people across the planet. The school brings together more than 30 different 'institutes', involving over 300 scholars. Their goal, according to James Martin, is to *"formulate new concepts, policies and technologies that will make the future a better place to be"*.

These various institutes conduct research programmes to identify and map out complex interdisciplinary-related future problems and to address the most pressing global challenges and opportunities of the 21st century. These programmes are grouped around four research areas: (1) technology and society, (2) energy and environment, (3) ethics and corporate governance, (4) health care and medical care. The research covers such broad topics as the future of the global food system, ageing, population growth, migration, energy and materials, climate change, geo-engineering, the human rights of future generations, nanotechnology, inequality, and innovation in healthcare. No other university anywhere in the world hosts a research organization like the Oxford Martin School.

Alongside the Oxford Martin School, *Green Templeton College* (GTC) also plays an important role in futures research. The GTC centralizes the research methodology on future thinking and complexity for all the different institutes of the Oxford Martin School. The GTC also administers the personal library and papers of Pierre Wack (1922-1997), one of the founders of scenario-based thinking and the first person to apply the ideas of Herman Kahn in practice. Together with the *Saïd Business School*, the GTC organizes the triennial Oxford Future Forum.[96] This has allowed Oxford to build up an impressive worldwide network of experts.

The University of Oxford is also involved in the development of strategic foresight and complexity thinking at the World Economic Forum (WEF), since many of the university's experts have participated in the Global Agenda Councils or the Global Strategic Foresight Community[97] of the WEF.

## Summary

1. The challenges imposed by the future contextual environment will impact strongly on countries, organizations and companies (*i.e.* the transactional environment). These challenges are complex and are likely to create increasing turbulence and uncertainty.

2. The challenges are linked to areas such as technology, public finance, demography, climate change, scarce natural resources, ecology and migration.

3. The turbulence will be caused by the mutual interdependencies of these factors (*cf.* complexity). In other words, the combination of a number of these factors will create a turbulent environment in which many problems will become wicked.

4. The world is not well prepared for resolving wicked problems in a turbulent environment:

   • Political decision-making at an international level is not powerful enough.
   • The methods, structures and institutions for decision-making in many countries are the result of very recent evolutions: increased labour productivity has brought great prosperity through efficient pragmatic thinking rather than through futures thinking.
   • This efficiency evolution has also brought centralization, resulting in a societal division between 'thinkers' and 'doers'. This results in the under-utilisation of talent in companies.

5. In order to tackle the challenges of the future, it is necessary to fully exploit all potential talents.

6. Most countries lack the methods needed to tackle these wicked problems. Fortunately, however, more and more governments are becoming aware of the necessity and urgency to invest in *futures thinking institutes*.

   • Where do strategic conversations take place in your country, debating the impact of the environment on your future prosperity?
   • What institute monitors the context in your country, making sense of the weak signals of change that will allow you to adjust in time (EWS)?

7. There is a clear link between prosperity, pro-activeness and anticipation (whether political or socio-economic) at a national level and the existence of formal institutes to foster futures thinking. Successful initiatives show a clear pattern and a similar approach: formal institutions, competent people in charge, interdisciplinary research, appropriate methodologies, reporting to the highest executive power. Among the leading countries, Singapore and the Nordic countries have the most advanced futures thinking systems, while the University of Oxford and the WEF play an important role as thought leaders.

# Chapter 7
# **Conclusion**

This book offers methods and presents arguments to encourage the introduction of futures thinking as an advanced strategic management approach for better decision-making in uncertain, complex and increasingly turbulent environments. It is not only useful to policy-makers, business leaders and captains of society, but also to all 'students' of strategy and anyone involved in decision preparation or support.

In Chapter 1, it was indicated that using the strategic scenario method for futures thinking is highly valuable, since it unveils hidden assumptions and hence makes explicit the hypotheses behind the mental models of the outside world (*i.e.* environment and context). Strategic scenarios are equally valuable for building *social capital*, which is essential for generating the trust that is necessary to reach consensus and mutual understanding on strategic agendas for long-term policy-making in government, business and society. Futures thinking also enables decision-makers to look at problems and find solutions in a 'safe' environment, namely *the future*. No one owns the future and, consequently, all options are open, politically neutral, discussable and uncommitted. Finding solutions to complex problems is much more difficult outside this safe environment. Many of the problems of today are caused by the rigidity of political power relations and predetermined negotiating positions, which make solutions far harder to define. Positioning or formulating these issues in the future detaches us from the gravity of the present that reduces everything to a matter of short-term (and often blurred, confusing and even personal) interest. Complex problems are often best solved at a higher conceptual level than the level where they are defined, occur or created.

Futures thinking is both a science and an art. As such, it is the ideal way to deal with 'wicked problems'. This special class of particularly pernicious and deep-rooted problems occurs in environments with increasing complexity, growing insecurity and an ever higher rhythm of change. The lack of information to fully define and understand wicked problems, resulting from the non-linear dynamic of their environmental interactions, make them hard to identify and even harder to eradicate. To cope with this situation, wicked problems have been made the focal point of a complex systems theory based on futures research. Gradually, more and more decision-makers in different industries and at different government levels are starting to acknowledge that our environment is becoming more and more turbulent. An increasing number of managers, directors and politicians are discovering to their cost that wicked problems can now occur on their watch. The global economic and financial systems are not only more complicated than in the past (due to the number of constituent elements), but are also growing more complex (due to the number of interconnections). As this complexity continues to multiply, so the non-linear effects of its internal interactions become more significant, leading to strategic shocks, strategic surprises, wildcards or even critical events.

The solutions will not be found in more sophisticated quantitative models or in more powerful computers, since we will never have sufficient information about the 'unknowable' future, which for self-evident reasons does not lend itself to *scientific* experiments designed to collect the data that is needed for our models. A more appropriate and intelligent way to approach this problem is to adapt our insights, decisions and opinions in accordance with new information *as and when it becomes available*. We can refer to this as *progressive insight*. In fact, this is precisely what *Bayes' theorem* tells us to do. The future is plural!

Donald Schön's research shows that relevant and important problems are frequently tricky, unclear and difficult to define. They often also come with 'fuzzy' solutions. Although viewed from a different perspective, this is also the conclusion reached by Emery and Trist: $L_{22}$ environmental connections can produce effects that are unexpected and unthinkable – until the unthinkable actually happens. These effects, named 'black swans'[99] by Nassim Taleb, have the potential to generate catastrophe. The mental models that we traditionally build, based on our experiences of the past, have very limited value in the face of these unexpected events. Worse, they restrict our responsiveness, because the unanticipated nature and large impact of 'black swans' are far beyond the scope of these traditional mental models, in which only 'white swans' live. Although black swans are, by definition, rare and unforeseen, their impact is so dramatic that it is worthwhile to invest in better methods to anticipate their uncertain arrival. In this way, we are better prepared for such future shocks when they do occur.

Obviously, we cannot identify all unexpected events in advance; consequently, uncertainty and risk can never be eliminated completely. This simply underlines the importance of devoting sufficient attention to the early detection and understanding of the weak signals that may signify that a 'black swan' is on its way. These signals can indicate the existence of latent uncertainties or risks in the environment, but they can also open the door to new opportunities. Creating a system that is able to capture and understand weak signals requires a process of *focused interpretation*[100] or *sensemaking* to be applied to possible future environments.

It is not essential (or even possible) for scenarios developed in this way to perfectly match what will actually happen in reality in the future. Scenarios are neither predictions nor forecasts. Nevertheless, thinking in a structural way about the future and going through the process of futures thinking increases the flexibility of strategic leaders and policy-makers at all levels. It is not so much the outcome of the strategic scenarios that is important, but rather the process of thinking and debating that the development of these scenarios entails. We must learn *with* and *from* the future.

In this way, futures thinking about the 'unthinkable' induces a positive behavioural change that promotes a proactive learning culture. Not only must we think *out of the box*, we must learn how to draw new boxes as well! These changes will generate an encouraging and positive flexibility that goes much further than the formal outcome of specific scenarios. This new culture will better prepare the organization to deal with future uncertainties, since it enhances the speed of reaction in turbulent environments and lays the foundation for a true learning organization.

In addition, *futures thinking* also forms the basis for entrepreneurship and *entrepreneurial thinking*. We define entrepreneurship as a systematic search for possible disruptions or changes in the environment in order to turn them into opportunities with the help of resources from others or leveraged through others. Early discovery and sensemaking of possible disruptions is therefore a huge advantage for those who can interpret the future, while forming a huge risk for those who cannot. In this respect, it is worth recalling the distinctions between predictability, risk and uncertainty that we demonstrated with Knight's experiment of the three bowls.

It is now more than 50 years since Bertrand de Jouvenel postulated that:

> *"A nation's future is determined too often by many small and dominant political groups with a very narrow vision of the future."*

He argued that this could be avoided if leaders – futures thinkers – could sketch idealistic images of what the future might bring, images that could then serve as a blueprint for the nation's future. This same fundamental idea is also known as *strategic intent* and was introduced into the strategic management literature by Gary Hamel and C.K. Prahalad in 1989.

Even so, caution is needed. Tetlock's 'hedgehogs' cling too stubbornly to a single dominant idea that they use to interpret all problems, creating bias and a lack of flexibility. This extremely limited view of a very narrowly defined environment can be disastrous in a rapidly changing world.

What will the future ultimately bring? No one can possibly know. But what we do know is that we should avoid putting too much trust in the adequacy of the old linear forecasting and modelling methods that were successful in the past. We need to critically evaluate their applicability and reframe them within a culture and through a process of future thinking. This is essential, because *classic management methods* and planning systems are only practical in situations where: (1) objectives are clear and stable, (2) all facets of the problem can be defined, and (3) it is possible to comprehend how outcomes will be affected. Important real life challenges, however, often have vague objectives, are unclear, have incomplete problem definitions, have unpredictable interactions, are highly complex, and occur in an environment that is uncertain and difficult to predict. In these circumstances, classic decision-making techniques are inadequate or even useless. In fact, they can sometimes create additional difficulties, since they might actually create the illusion that the organization is on the right track when the very opposite is the case.

An important feature of complex and turbulent environments is that the available information is incomplete and will always remain incomplete: these are Donald Rumsfeld's *unknown unknowns*! This kind of turbulent environment requires a pragmatic and eclectic approach. This implies that for highly complex problems *probing* is required and action is needed: it is important to *do something*. In the absence of information, it is impossible to plan, but by taking action we can learn from the response, findings or feedback of others, and so develop a better understanding of the problem. Writing a book, conducting a research study or establishing an innovative corporation are all better than making plans based on erratic or non-validated information. Getting started is the crucial thing. Armed with a learning mindset and a problem-testing approach, you can then monitor and adjust your progress as you go. *Practice makes perfect*. Perhaps this is the hardest part: having the audacity to think, to experiment and to make mistakes at executive committee, board or cabinet level. You need to have the courage and the wisdom to acknowledge that complexity does not allow absolute mastery, which makes advance planning difficult or even, on occasions, impossible. This realization can be frightening for the majority of managers – but it is the only way to develop a learning organization.

Throughout this book we have advocated futures thinking as an innovative way to institutionalize new cultural values, so that leaders can be better prepared and perhaps eventually can even anticipate or reduce the impact of future shocks. In this respect, a key role is reserved for politics, universities and companies.

In most advanced thought-leading countries in the field of foresight today, political leaders have established an *'institute for the future'* to facilitate and encourage the building of a proactive and future-oriented culture. By stimulating the use of futures-thinking methods and processes, they hope to develop policies that anticipate and/or avoid major problems, while simultaneously creating new opportunities that can generate more national wealth. The examples of Singapore and the Scandinavian countries (*cf.* chapter 6) are exemplary in this respect. There is still a great need for more futures institutes in many different countries and it is essential that these institutes are open to new and innovative thinking! Experience over many years has shown that the key success factors are openness and the ability to learn. This requires continuous political attention, talent and courage, since in times of uncertainty it is sometimes easier to follow short-term populism than to remain firm behind the policies and investments suggested by future scenario planning. Visionary political leaders give nations the institutions and administrations that will provide for prosperity in the future (*cf.* Acemoglu & Robinson, 2012).

The universities can greatly assist in this process by participating in the social debate on relevant future-oriented questions. An interdisciplinary orientation in research and teaching on the basis of futures thinking can make a powerful and relevant contribution in this respect. The establishment of more futures research institutes would highlight this important new role, which all universities should take up.

In similar fashion, business can organize strategic futures debates on the basis of well-constructed scenarios, asking the question: how do we prepare our sectors and enterprises for this uncertain and turbulent future? Many business leaders in organizations of all sizes are still not trained to deal with or develop strategies for volatile and complex environments. They intuitively feel that their existing methods and tools are no longer wholly adequate, but have so far failed to master the alternatives provided by futures thinking. Of course, pragmatism and flexibility certainly have advantages, but they also have limitations as well. They frequently offer short-term solutions and hence are ineffective to anticipate long-term disruptive challenges. We need to arm our business leaders with something more effective.

The findings in Chapter 2 showed that in today's economy more than half the value creation of an enterprise is realized through its context. Strategy thinking should therefore incorporate more futures research findings and develop new methods that take greater account of the impact of context uncertainty. At the present time, very few business schools actually deliver answers to these questions or even carry out academic research into this crucial topic. It nevertheless is essential that such further research should be conducted, since it will assist business leaders in an uncertain future to take the investment decisions that are vital for innovation and growth.

Boards of directors also have an important role to play. Research shows that boards, especially in turbulent times, find it difficult to contribute to comprehensive and robust strategy plans and policies. Many companies do indeed have a propensity to draw up their 'strategic plan' on the basis of largely meaningless extrapolations from annual budgets or multi-year financial data projections. A lack of know-how only partly explains this problem. Selecting competent independent board members for strategic committees in keeping with the principles of 'corporate governance' still tends to be the exception rather than the rule, but it remains an absolute criterion for the successful implementation of futures thinking. Given these constraints, it is not surprising that companies who have already introduced a culture of strategic debates are few and far between. But those who have done it have built up a significant competitive advantage.

In one of his last lectures, Professor C.K. Prahalad (1941-2010) argued that in addition to the productivity, quality, speed, re-engineering and innovation of their business models, competitive advantage in the years ahead will be gained by the companies that are able to create structures capable of making decisions in turbulent environments, *i.e.* environments with great uncertainty.

With this is mind, we are convinced of the need to establish what we call 'strategy-driven companies' (SDC) or 'strategy-oriented companies' (SOC). We define these companies, enterprises or institutions as organizations that capture environmental information in a systematic way and use it in an equally systematic way for strategic debates and for testing and challenging strategic options and investments. SOCs must add to their existing corporate governance committees (*i.e.* finance, audit, HRM or strategy) a new committee that we call the *futures committee*. This new futures committee can either replace or be complementary to the strategy committee and its responsibilities will include: (1) initiating strategic debates, (2) provide a sounding board for the CEO's strategy, (3) initiating projects and processes on sensemaking, (4) testing, assessing and investigating the robustness of strategic investments, (5) installing discovery-driven planning, and (6) installing an EWS system. The futures committee will also discuss innovation, new markets, capacity expansions, and mergers and acquisitions. It sounds simple? Perhaps, but it isn't – otherwise it would be too easy to copy and hence could never create a truly sustainable competitive advantage. In reality, once a business has mastered strategic conversations through its futures committee, it will be possible for it to develop into something that very few other businesses have so far been able to achieve: an organization that can adapt to turbulence and rapid change and responds more quickly and more flexibly to opportunities than its competitors. This will be the killer app of the 21$^{st}$ century.

If this book has convinced the reader of the need to tackle future challenges in a different way and has led to the realization that most existing quantitative decision-making methods are seriously flawed when applied to turbulent environments, then we can consider our mission a success. The next important step is to examine how this can be successfully implemented in practice. The creation of institutes for the future at national level or futures committees at board of directors level is certainly a first step worth considering. But above all, we need leaders who have the wisdom, courage and openness of mind to place their faith in thinking futures. *Sapere Aude!*

# Glossary

**Backcasting:** is a method by which the possible futures scenarios are first determined without taking into account constraints. From these possible futures the desired futures or the futures that should be avoided are selected. Only then are the strategies developed to achieve the desired future or to avoid the undesired future (*cf.* forecast).

**Cross-impact analysis** (CIA): is an analysis in which the impact of trends or events are mutually identified and evaluated. *Cf.* the European Joint Research Center on CIA: http://forlearn.jrc.ec.europa.eu/guide/2_scoping/meth_cross-impact-analysis.htm (Accessed 16 December 2015).

**Delphi technique:** this involves a pool of experts investigating a problem that situates itself in the future. During the process, the experts have no contact with each other. Their opinions are collected through questionnaires. The aim is to reach a consensus between these different opinions when evaluating the questionnaires, because certain factors are subjective. The respondents are questioned individually and possibly in different rounds. The results from the previous rounds form the input for the questionnaires of the following rounds.

**Early warning systems** (EWS) (Signposts): are systems that recognize early signals that can indicate an increased likelihood that a specific scenario will happen.

**Forecast:** is a quantitative approach that estimates in advance (on the basis of experts or expert systems) or calculates (through models or extrapolation, including statistics, regression analysis, *etc.*) knowledge about a future situation. When making predictions, developments in the past are extended to the future on the basis of assumptions about which extrapolated trends will actually happen.

**Future screening**: See Future scanning

**Futurism:** is a science and an art that tries to obtain insight into the future with the aim of identifying the causes that will affect (future) changes in the PEST (see PEST-analysis).

**Horizon Scanning**: is estimating the external, turbulent and sometimes complex environment of an organization with regard to its competitive and enterprising (or strategic) behaviour, combined with the political, economic and environmental, social and technological influences (see also PEST-analysis). The external environment consists of all conditions and forces that affect the strategic options and operational activities of the company.

**Open systems:** are entities that interact with the environment. Conversely, closed systems are isolated and have no interaction with the environment.

**PEST analysis:** is an acronym for four key factors influencing the environment of the organization. These factors are: (P) political, (E) economic and ecological, (S) social, (T) technological (*cf.* horizon scanning). There exist other acronyms like STEEP – PESTEL – SPECTRE encompassing (E) ecological, (C) cultural, and (L) law.

**Prediction:** is a statement about the future; saying what will happen.

**Risk management:** is a discipline to estimate operational and strategic risk and to develop strategies to manage these external (and internal) risk factors.

**Scenario:** is the application of a systematic method to estimate future risks and uncertainties. It is a combination of estimates of what can happen and assumptions of what could happen. These are no predictions or select assumptions of what will happen. A good description of scenarios has been given by Kees van der Heijden, who refers to scenario work in organizations: "*an instrument (a 'tool'), both in the sense of process and content, to tackle the inherent uncertainty of the future and to create adaptive organizations.*"

With 'process', van der Heijden refers to the method that enables an organization to carry out research and to discuss its implications in a strategic conversation. With 'content', he refers to the fact that the success of any organization depends on unique insights and discoveries that the organization can generate to be different from others, and the fact that scenarios can produce this.

**Scenario-based thinking** or scenario planning: is a method to engage in future thinking. All possible futures or goals are investigated, without taking into account possible constraints or difficulties.

**Scenario thinking:** See scenario-based thinking.

**Sensemaking** (interpreting): is giving meaning or sense to a perception or event.

**Scenario learning** is the application of scenario methods to improve the learning behaviour of individuals or organizations.

**Strong signals:** are generally accepted assumptions (*e.g.* the current changes in demographics or the further increase in e-business), which relate to an industry or market. These signals are clear and sufficiently specific, so that the organization can prepare by calculating the impact or by developing specific plans in response.

**Strategic conversations:** See strategic debates

**Strategic foresight**: is a qualitative approach to achieve a better understanding of the future (unlike predictions). In an organization, far-sighted thinking is part of strategy development in the medium to long term (eight to twenty years, or even fifty years). This approach aims to transform the challenges of the future into innovations by increasing the creativity and the learning capacities of the organization.

**Strategic shock** (strategic surprise): is a suddenly emerging issue with great impact and is therefore of significant strategic importance. It creates problems for the organization that are either new or problems in an area where the organization has little experience. In both cases, the issue requires immediate action. Such situations cannot be solved with normal procedures and systems (also known as wild cards or critical events).

**Strategic scenario planning**: using scenarios to test the robustness of strategic decisions or strategic options.

**Strategic management/policy**: is a planning process to manage the organization with a view to the future, in order to transform threats from the environment into opportunities (time horizon: five to twenty years, in some cases more).

**System analysis**: is an explicit and formal investigation, which is conducted in order to help the decision-maker take better decisions than would otherwise be the case. The typical characteristics of a problem situation where system analysis is used include the complexity of the problem and uncertainty about the outcome of any reasonable decision relating to the action to follow. System analysis typically consists of a combination of the following elements: identification and re-identification of the objectives, constraints and alternatives; an examination of the possible consequences of various alternatives in terms of costs, benefits and risks; a comparative schedule from which the decision-maker can choose alternatives to reach a reasonable end-choice.

**Systems thinking**: is a problem-solving method in which the problem is seen as an element within a larger whole, so that the various elements are interrelated.

**Future**: is the time before us. Since the future involves an element of uncertainty, organizations try to prepare themselves to deal with this uncertainty.

**Future scanning**: is a process in the contemporary approach to business strategy, whereby strategic conversations based on long-term scenarios (using strong and weak signals) are held. It is the first stage in the analysis of the situation that leads to the selection of a final strategy. Strategic thinking is stimulated by this part of the process and it also makes companies aware of possible discontinuities. It further encourages organizations to adopt a longer time horizon (longer than the typical three or five year plans) in their strategy development. The goal is to increase innovation capacity, to better identify opportunities and to better anticipate potential threats.

**Future thinking:** makes solid studies and analysis about possible alternative futures. There are several methods that can be employed to conduct future thinking (see forecasting, foresight, Delphi technique, backcasting, system analysis, cross-impact analysis).

**Future projection:** is a certain vision of the future, based on specific information and a collection of logical assumptions.

**Trends-impact analysis** (TIA): is a method by which historical trends are extrapolated to allow future thinking. Afterwards, experts look at possible deviations.

**Foresight thinking:** See: strategic foresight.

**Wicked problems** are problems that are very difficult or even impossible to solve. The concept of wicked problems was initially proposed by Horst W.J. Rittel and Melvin M. Webber (1973). Rittel was professor of the science of design and planning issues at the University of California in Berkeley. He characterized poorly defined scheduling problems as wicked (fuzzy circular argument, aggressive, *etc.*). He contrasted this with the *tame problems* (well-defined problems, such as in mathematics, chess or puzzling).

**Weak signals:** are the least accessible (hardest to identify) observations in environmental scanning, which can disrupt an organization's strategic planning. Weak signals are ill-defined and/or not (yet) affiliated with a specific industry or market. They contain threats and opportunities and will continue to evolve over time. The identification and the correct interpretation of these weak signals is vital to the success and even the survival of an organization. Since the information is vague and its future development unclear, the answer for dealing with the situation will only be in partial focus.

**Black swan:** the term 'black swan' dates back to an incident when Dutch explorers reported in 1697 that they had seen black swans in Western Australia. The report was ridiculed, because at the time only white swans were known. Science philosophers use the term today to point out that induction based on previous empirical knowledge or events can lead to wrong conclusions. Author Nassim Nicholas Taleb used the term as the title of his 2008 book, in which he described the blunders made as a result of the false knowledge, incorrect theories or complete ignorance of financial experts, which brought the markets to the brink of the abyss.

# Acknowledgements

We are obliged to our colleagues, friends and mentors from Oxford for their tutorship and for sharing their wisdom with us: Professor Sir David Watson (1949-2015) who we miss greatly, Professor Ian Goldin, Professor Rafael Ramirez, Professor John Lennox, Professor Steve Rayner and Dr Angela Wilkinson.

We are equally indebted for the insights shared during our many conversations with our colleagues and students from the Defence College (Royal Military Academy) and Ghent University, our friends and colleagues from the Royal Academy of Belgium, the members of the Global Strategic Foresight Community and the Global Agenda Councils on complexity and foresight of the World Economic Forum and last but not least our teachers, colleagues and friends of the Oxford Futures Forum and the Oxford Scenario Program (Saïd Business School).

We are especially grateful to Dr Carine Boonen, Count Paul Buysse CBE CMG, Professor Marc Cools, Professor Mark Eyskens, Lieutenant General Eddy Testelmans, Kristel Van der Elst, Count Herman Van Rompuy and General Joseph Van den Put for their leadership, courage and persistency in bringing future thinking to the highest levels of decision-making in Belgium.

D.P.G. and B.T.

June 2016

Green Templeton College, Oxford
Ghent University, Ghent
Royal Military Academy, Brussels

# About the Authors

**Derrick GOSSELIN** is professor at the Royal Military Academy of Belgium, where he heads the advanced management and strategic leadership programme of its Defence College. He is also full professor of strategy and marketing at Ghent University and an associate fellow of both Green Templeton College and the Oxford Martin School at the University of Oxford. His research focuses on strategic decision-making in complex and uncertain environments applied to strategy, innovation, intelligence and technology marketing. He is founder and chair of the Centre for Futures Research at Ghent University and Member of the WEF's Global Strategic Foresight Community. He was previously Member of the WEF's Global Agenda Council on Foresight and on Complexity.

He studied engineering, economics and business administration at Ghent University, Vlerick Business School, INSEAD and the University of Oxford. He is Fellow of the Royal Belgian Academy (KVAB), Academia Europaea and Honorary Fellow of High Hill College at KU Leuven. He serves on the Board of Governors of the Royal Higher Institute for Defence, the Belgian Nuclear Research Center SCK.CEN, the von Karman Institute for Fluid Dynamics, the World Energy Council (Belgium) and ECSA.

Prior to joining Academia, he spent over 25 years in international senior executive positions in industry, government and politics.

**Bruno TINDEMANS** is CEO of *Syntra Vlaanderen*, the Flemish agency providing professional education for over 85.000 participants. Bruno is also a Senior Research Fellow and co-founder of the Centre for Futures Research at Ghent University and visiting lecturer at the Saïd Business School, University of Oxford. His research interest is in entrepreneurial renewal and strategic foresight development in turbulent environments.

Prior to that, Bruno was the founding dean of Flanders Business School/KULeuven from 1999 until 2012, creating the first accredited MBA school in Belgium with a focus on entrepreneurship and spinning-off more than 120 new ventures. Flanders Business School became the subject of international research for new business models for future MBA schools, following a 2009 evaluation report by the Harvard Commission on Management Training.

Bruno holds Master degrees in commercial and financial sciences, consular sciences (international relations) and business administration (MBA) and a Doctorate of Business Administration (DBA) from Cranfield University, School of Management. He is alumnus of the Saïd Business School, Oxford University.
Bruno's recent books relate to corporate entrepreneurship and strategic foresight.

# Notes

1   www.smithschool.ox.ac.uk

2   *Tractatus Logico-Philosophicus* (*cf.* Tractatus).

3   A future Nobel laureate for physics (1965), Richard Feynman (1918-1988) was not even fifteen years old when he wrote in bold letters in his diary on first encountering the Euler formula: "the most remarkable formula in maths" *Euler's formula*: Napier's constant or Euler's number $e = 2.718\,281\ldots$ (an irrational number) raised to the power $\pi = 3.141\,592\ldots$ (another irrational number) multiplied by the square root of (-1) being $i = \sqrt{-1}$ (an imaginary and complex number), plus 1 (an integer), equals 0 (zero is at the same time a natural, a rational, a real, and a complex number representing nothing).

4   From the 1930s onwards, the system theory was developed by (Karl) Ludwig von Bertalanffy as a multi-disciplinary science to investigate the characteristics of reality through systems. This led to research into complex dynamical systems, better known as chaos theory. The system theory also teaches us the limitations of our models when they are confronted with dynamic (turbulent) environments and so they become unstable, unreliable and/or unpredictable.

5   Sensemaking is the process by which people give sense to a particular experience. The term was first introduced in organization studies by Karl Weick in 1988 and was described in detail in his book: *Sensemaking in Organizations* (1995).

6   Major General Carl Philipp Gottfried von Clausewitz was director of the *Preußische Kriegsakademie* – Prussian Staff College or War College – in Berlin from 1818 until 1830.

7   General Helmuth Johannes Ludwig von Moltke was Chief of the German General Staff from 1906 to 1914.

8   One of the most famous post-war speeches was given by Sir Winston S. Churchill at Westminster College, Fulton, Missouri (U.S.) on 5 March 1946 and was attended by President Harry S. Truman. The speech is officially entitled *The Sinews of Peace* but is better known as the *Iron Curtain* speech. http://en.wikisource.org/wiki/Sinews_of_Peace (Accessed 20 December 2015).

9   RAND was an initiative of General Henry H. Arnold, Commander-in-Chief of the U.S. Air Force, together with his friend Donald W. Douglas, founder and owner of the eponymous aircraft company. In 1948, RAND became an independent non-profit organization (www.rand.org)

10  The Douglas Aircraft Company merged with the McDonnell Aircraft Corporation to become the McDonnell-Douglas Corporation in 1967, which subsequently merged with Boeing in 1997.

11  This is the same Dr Theodore von Kármán, who in 1956 founded an institute for training and research in aerodynamics for NATO countries at Sint-Genesius-Rode near Brussels. After his death in 1963, the institute became world-renowned as the *Von Karman Institute for Fluid Dynamics* (www.vki.ac.be).

12 The members were soon called Whiz Kids because of their brilliance and youthful age. Some well-known members were: John von Neumann, founder of game theory and modern computer architecture; Robert McNamara, who later became Minister of Defence under President John F. Kennedy; Oliver E. Williamson, Nobel Prize winner in Economics (2009) for transaction cost economics; John F. Nash, Nobel Prize winner in Economics (1994) for non-cooperative game theory (*cf.* Nash-equilibrium).

13 General George S. Patton (1885-1945) summarized this problem of group thinking in his famous quote: "*If everyone is thinking alike, then somebody isn't thinking*".

14 Herman Kahn is probably unknown to most people. His ideas for a hypothetical 'Doomsday Machine' that might destroy the whole world automatically when attacked, made him a model for the character of Dr Strangelove in the eponymous 1964 film by Stanley Kubrick. The word 'escalation' is also attributed to him and was first used in his book *On Escalation* in 1965.

15 www.lampsacus.com/documents/CROSSIMPACT.pdf (Accessed 20 December 2015)

16 Quote from Gaston Berger from his article *Sciences Humaines et Prévisions*, printed in February 1957 in *la Revue des Deux Mondes*: "*Notre civilisation s'arrache avec peine à la fascination du passé. De l'avenir, elle ne fait que rêver et, lorsqu'elle élabore des projets qui ne sont plus de simples rêves, elle les dessine sur une toile où c'est encore le passé qui se projette. Elle est rétrospective, avec entêtement. Il lui faut devenir 'prospective'.*"

17 Maurice Béjart (1927-2007) is the stage name of Maurice Jean Berger. Mr. Berger took the name Béjart as an homage to Armande Béjart, wife of Jean-Baptiste Poquelin – also known as Molière (1622-1673).

18 'Futuribles' is the contraction of *futures possibles* (www.futuribles.com).

19 Pierre Massé was elected member of the *Académie des sciences morales et politiques*, one of the five academies of the *Institut de France*. He engraved his ceremonial sword with the inscription: *Comprendre, Construire, Convaincre* (*i.e.* Comprehend, Construct, Convince).

20 In 2006, the *Bureau français du Plan* was reorganized to become the *Centre d'analyse stratégique*, which in 2013 was further transformed with extended responsibilities to become the *Commissariat général à la stratégie et à la prospective* – known for short as *France Stratégie* – reporting directly to the prime minister (www.strategie.gouv.fr).

21 The notion *wicked problem* was first used in 1973 by Professor Horst W.J. Rittel (1930-1990) and Professor Melvin M. Webber (1920-2006), both from the University of California at Berkeley. They identified 10 characteristics of this type of problem. A wicked problem is actually a problem that is very hard and sometimes even impossible to solve, because information is lacking. Wicked problems often come with a number of built-in contradictions, making it even more difficult to recognize them for what they are. Additionally, because of interdependencies and interactions, trying to solve one part of the problem can sometimes create new problems. Often a problem of this type is only understood and defined once the solution(s) are known.

22 This performance was measured by Return on Assets (ROA). ROA is calculated by dividing a company's annual earnings by its total assets. ROA gives an idea of how efficient management is at using its assets (or total invested capital) to generate profits.

23 It is interesting to compare the concepts of the 'wicked problem' and the 'fog of war'. The latter was introduced by Carl von Clausewitz (*cf. On War*). It can be described as a situation of incomplete, dubious and often completely erroneous information, combined with high levels of fear, doubt and excitement.

24 This problem and approach was very well summarized and clearly expressed by Peter F. Drücker (1909-2005):"*The greatest danger in times of turbulence is not the turbulence; it is to act with yesterday's logic*".

25 Taxonomy: the science or practice used to make a classification of things or concepts, including the principles that underlie such classification. From the ancient Greek word *taxinomos*, a combination of *taxis* (τάξις) meaning 'order' and *nomos* (νόμος) meaning 'law' or 'science'.

26 Actually, it is past behaviour over a long period of time and observed in many diverse situations that is the excellent predictor and not behaviour observed in only a few situations and all of the same type.

27 Philip E. Tetlock has been a member of the Faculty of the University of Pennsylvania since 2011, as the Leonore Annenberg University Professor of Psychology and Management. He also teaches at the School of Arts and Sciences and at the Wharton Business School.

28 Sherman Kent started his career as a history professor at Yale in 1935. He joined the Research and Analysis Branch of the Coordinator of Information (COI) in 1941. The COI became the Office of Strategic Services (OSS). The OSS became the CIA. He is often described as "the father of intelligence analysis". The key word in Kent's work is *estimate* that he defines as: "estimating is what you do when you do not know".

29 The Brier Score $BS = \dfrac{1}{N} \sum\limits_{i=1}^{N} (p_i - o_i)^2$

$N$ is the number of forecasts to be tested. $p_i$ are the probabilities associated with the forecasted events. The observations $o_i$ of what actually happened are all binary, 1 if the event occurred and 0 if it didn't.

30 Tetlock uses this terminology based on the essay *The Hedgehog and the Fox* written in 1953 by the British-Latvian-born Oxford philosopher, founder of Wolfson College, Sir Isaiah Berlin (1909-1997). The title is a reference to a fragment attributed to the ancient Greek poet Archilochus of Pharos (c. 680 B.C. – c. 645 B.C.): "*the fox knows many things, but the hedgehog knows one big thing*" (πόλλ' οἶδ' ἀλώπηξ, ἀλλ' ἐχῖνοςἓνμέγα).

31 For an analysis of the collapse of the Fortis Group, see: Fassin Y., Gosselin D. (2011) *Journal of Business Ethics*.

32 http://www.nato.int/docu/speech/2002/s020606g.htm (Accessed 20 December 2015).

33 Dr Dylan Evans introduces the interesting concept of *Risk Intelligence*. He defines Risk Intelligence (RQ) as the ability to estimate probabilities accurately. People with high risk intelligence tend to make better predictions than those with low RQ (www.projectionpoint.com).

34 Frank Knight introduced the concept of *Knightian uncertainty* in economics. Knightian uncertainty is a risk that is immeasurable and therefore not possible to calculate.

35    The Chicago School of Economics is part of the Department of Economics at the University of Chicago. This department is considered one of the world's foremost economics departments. It has produced more Nobel Prizes in Economics (NPE) than any other university. Milton Friedman (NPE 1976) and George Stigler (NPE 1982) were both students of Frank Knight. Ronald Coase (NPE 1991), founder of transaction cost economics (TCE), Gary S. Becker (NPE 1992) (cf. freakonomics), Eugene Fama (NPE 2013) and Lars Peter Hansen (NPE 2013) were all members of the Chicago School. The Chicago School is known for its rejection of Keynesianism in favour of Monetarism until the mid-1970s, when it turned to new classical macroeconomics, heavily based on the concept of rational expectations.

36    Digital text of the book is available at https://mises.org/library/risk-uncertainty-and-profit [accessed 20 December 2015].

37    A Black Swan is defined as an unexpected event with very low probability of occurring but with very high impact when it actually occurs, such as the financial crisis of 2008.

38    This is exactly what probability theory tells us to do. We know that estimating a probability distribution using sampling will only reduce the error margin or increase the confidence level if we increase the number of samples $n$. So the more candies we draw out of the bowl, the more accurately we can estimate the theoretical distribution. Meanwhile, *other things* can still happen.

39    This paragraph is based on an article co-authored by D. Gosselin: *Perspectives on a Hyperconnected World: Insights from the Science of Complexity*, World Economic Forum, GAC Complexity, 2013.

40    A learning organization consciously promotes the learning of all its members in order to continually transform itself and adapt to its environment. Peter Senge (1990, p. 3) defines this as organizations where people continually develop their ability to achieve the results they truly desire, where new and expansive patterns of thinking are nurtured, where there is freedom to pursue joint aspirations and where people constantly learn how to learn together.

41    Other anagrams used in the strategic management literature are PEST, PESTLE and PESTLED, while in marketing literature STEEP, STEEPLE, STEEPLED or SPECTRE are more frequently used.

42    For an overview of the academic literature on the matching concept cf. Gosselin D.P. (2002). *Strategic Account Management*. Faculty of Economics and Business Administration, Ghent University, Belgium.

43    Emery, F. E., Trist E.L. (1965), The causal texture of organization environments, *Human Relations*, 18 (1), 21-32.

44    Later, in addition to the four causal textures of Emery and Trist, three additional ambient types were defined: *hyper turbulence* by McCann and Selsky, the *whirlpool environment* (vortical environment) by Babüroğlu and in 2011 the *feral futures* by Ramirez and Ravetz.

45    Where the products offered are fairly identical: similar clutter at a flea market or similar carrots and turnips at a vegetable market.

46    Game theory is a mathematical theory of strategic decision-making. It models human interactive behaviour in situations of conflict and cooperation where decisions must

be taken. The founders of game theory were three exceptionally gifted professors at Princeton University: John von Neumann (1903-1957), Oskar Morgenstern (1902-1977) and John Forbes Nash, Jr. (1928-2015). We mention here the *Nash-equilibrium*: this is a strategic choice of one player during a game, which is such that the strategy of each player is the best response to the actions of all other players. The Nash equilibrium redeems us from the circle that starts with *"I think that he thinks that I think..."*. The 2001 film of Sylvia Nasar's book, *A Beautiful Mind*, tells the story of Professor John F. Nash, winner of the Nobel Prize for Economics in 1994.

47   The concept 'open innovation' was introduced by Henry Chesbrough, director of the Center for Open Innovation, University of California at Berkeley. In Europe, his ideas have been further developed by Wim Vanhaverbeke at Hasselt University in Belgium.

48   *The CEO Report*. www.sbs.ox.ac.uk/sites/default/files/Press_Office/Docs/The-CEO-Report-Final.pdf (Accessed 21 December 2015).

49   www.foresight-platform.eu (Accessed 20 December 2015).

50   For an extensive description of the most frequently used methods for futures research, we refer to the *Online Foresight Guide* of the *Institute for Prospective Technological Studies* (IPTS) of the *Joint Research Centre* of the European Commission: http://forlearn. jrc.ec.europa.eu/guide/4_methodology/index.htm (Accessed 21 December 2015).

51   *The Exploits of Espadián or The Adventures of Espadián* is the fifth book in a series of Spanish chivalric romance novels written by Garcia Rodriguez de Montalvo, probably publish in Seville in 1496.

52   In *Las Sergas de Esplandián*, Rodríguez described a mythical *Island of California* as being west of the Indies:
     *"Know, that on the right hand of the Indies there is an island called California very*
     *close to the side of the Terrestrial Paradise; and it is peopled by black women, without*
     *any man among them, for they live in the manner of Amazons... Their arms are*
     *made of solid gold... on the whole island there is no other metal than gold."*
     The novel was highly influential in motivating Hernán Cortés and other explorers to discover the '*island*', which they believed lay along the west coast of North America. In 1539, Francisco de Ulloa, sailing under the commission of Cortés, explored the Gulf of California and the coast of Baja California peninsula, determining that it was indeed a peninsula, and not an island. Nevertheless, the cartographic misconception of California as an island persisted on many European maps well into the 18th century.

53   The philosophy of science makes a distinction between the 'predictive' and the 'explanatory' power of a theory. The more powerful a theory, the higher its predictive power and the better its predictions can be tested (*cf.* falsifiability). A theory without predictive power cannot be tested; hence, it cannot be verified if the theory is true or not. It is at best a supposition and at worst a piece of pseudoscience.

54   The title of his book – A *Farwell to Alms: A Brief Economic History of the World* – is a play on words on the title of Ernest Hemingway's novel *A Farewell to Arms*, published in 1929.

55   Former CIA analyst, Richards J. Heuer, Jr. developed a method called *Analysis of Competing Hypotheses* (ACH) to think about complex problems when the available information is incomplete or ambiguous. This method is elaborated in his book *Psychology of Intelligence Analysis*, published in 1999. A support software ACH 2.0.5 is available from

the Palo Alto Research Center (PARC) at http://www2.parc.com/istl/projects/ach/ach.html (Accessed 25 December 2015).

56 Orthogonality is a mathematical term used to describe the relations of non-overlapping, uncorrelated or independent objects. In statistics and probability theory, independent variables that affect a particular dependent variable are said to be orthogonal if they are uncorrelated. In *taxonomy*, an orthogonal classification is one in which no item is a member of more than one group; that is, the classifications are mutually exclusive.

57 The relationship between the production and distribution costs of solar energy and the price of oil are most probably not completely independent. After all, when oil prices increase, we will accelerate the search for alternatives.

58 Michel Godet is a professor of *industrial prospective thinking* at the Conservatoire National des Arts et Metiers (CNAM) in Paris, one of the famous French *Grandes Écoles* (www.cnam.fr) (Accessed 13 March 2016).

59 Current initiatives are being taken by *Planetary Resources – the Asteroid Mining Company* (www.planetaryresources.com), a venture of James Cameron and Google billionaires Larry Page and Eric Schmidt. They are looking into the possible tapping of extra-terrestrial resources, including helium-3. Others are *Moon Express* (www.moonexpress.com), selected by NASA as its partner to develop a robotic spacecraft to allow the resources of the moon to be mined. They won the Google Lunar XPRIZE™ in 2010 and technology demonstrator missions are planned as of 2015. The Chinese government is planning similar actions.

60 SWOT is the abbreviation for strengths, weaknesses, opportunities and threats.

61 www.montfleur.co.za

62 Adam Kahane is since 2009 an associate fellow of the *Institute for Science, Innovation and Society* (InSIS) at the University of Oxford's Saïd Business School. InSIS is one of the institutes of the *Oxford Martin School*.

63 Adam Kamane is currently an Associate Fellow of the Saïd Business School, University of Oxford.

64 Ariëns H., Van Genugten L. (2010) Interview: Adam Kahane, ISOline, March 2010.

65 "*What is necessary is never ridiculous.*"

66 In 2010, Australia decided to provide high speed fibre broadband access (100 MBit/s) to 90% of all houses. By doing so nearly 100% of its population was connected to a world class high speed communications network. This implied an investment of $ 43 billion U.S. dollars in 2010.

67 Some Americans are of the latter so convinced that they now already allow themselves to be frozen after their deaths, in the hope that future generations may awaken them to life again.

68 On 6 March 2015, the U.S. had a total public debt of $18.15 trillion or a debt-to-GDP ratio of 103.2% with a 2014 GDP of $17.25 trillion. Approximately $6.1 trillion of the total public debt was owned by foreign investors, the largest of which was the People's Republic of China, with about $1.3 trillion.

69 Teulings C. & Baldwin R. Eds. (2014) *Secular Stagnation: Facts, Causes, and Cures* www.voxeu.org/sites/default/files/Vox_secular_stagnation.pdf (Accessed 21 December 2015).

70  Acemoglu and Robinson refute partially the causes given to explain differences in wealth between countries as presented by Jared Diamond (climate, geography, bacteriology); Ian Morris (mainly geography, but also climate, migration, hunger, disease and the collapse of government) and Niall Ferguson (the six killer-apps of prosperity for the West: competition, the scientific revolution, property rights, modern medicine, consumer society and work ethic).

71  The People's Republic of China held $ 1.3 trillion of the U.S. total public debt on 6 March 2015. China is the largest foreign owner of U.S. public debt.

72  The average monthly salary per capita in China in an urban area in 2013 was $350, according to the National Bureau of Statistics (www.stats.gov.cn/english). Chinese minimum wages are two or three times the level of their Indian counterparts, and even higher when welfare payments are added. China now has one of the highest employment costs in emerging Asia.

73  Official name: New Influenza A (H1N1).

74  It was, in fact, a gene, called NDM-1 or New Delhi-Metallo-1. When it is affected by a bacterium, it creates an enzyme that makes the bacterium virtually immune to the most common antibiotics. In this way, the bacterium becomes multi-resistant.

75  For a scenario analysis on this subject *cf.* Gosselin D.P & Leysen J. (2008).

76  In its original form, Arrhenius' greenhouse law reads as follows: "*if the quantity of carbonic acid [$CO_2$] increases in geometric progression, the augmentation of the temperature will increase nearly in arithmetic progression.*"

77  Interview by Frank Eltman, on 26 May 2012, Associate Press NY: *Evolution will soon be history.* www.nbcnews.com/id/47577163/ns/technology_and_science-science/#. VRt6YfmsWL2 (Accessed 21 December 2015)

78  www.ippc.ch

79  *e.g.* contributions by Frederick Taylor, Henri Fayol, Frank & Lilian Gilbreth, Michael Hammer.

80  Perhaps we should not underestimate the important role played by politics in the creation of this enormous improvement in prosperity.

81  We refer here to the important report of Prins & Rayner (2010).

82  Since 2012, Belgium holds the world record for the most number of days needed to form a government: 541 days.

83  Nikolas Stern FRS FBA (Lord Stern of Brentford) is a British economist and academic. From 2000 to 2003, he was the chief economist of the World Bank. From 2003 to 2007, he was an economic advisor to H.M. Treasury. He became world famous after the publication of his report: *The Stern Review on the Economics of Climate Change* in October 2006. Since 2007, he has been a full professor at the London School of Economics and Political Science (LSE).

84  The term 'contained depression' was originally coined by David Levy and S. Jay Levy in 1990. They are both affiliated to the *Levy Economics Institute* of Bard College, Annandale-on Hudson, New York.

85  Einstein, A. (1948), A Message to Intellectuals. In: *Albert Einstein*, Green J. (Ed.), 2003, p. 52.

86  Officially, the Nobel Prize in Economics does not exist. What is commonly referred

to as the Nobel Prize in Economics is actually the *Swedish National Bank Prize in Economic Sciences in Memory of Alfred Nobel*. This prize is awarded under the same conditions and by the same Royal Swedish Academy of Sciences that also grants the Nobel Prizes. It is awarded at the same prize giving ceremony in Stockholm, on the 10 December, the anniversary of Nobel's death.

87    This theory explains that people are not able to analyse complex situations when the future consequences are uncertain. We wrongly overestimate the chance that small opportunities will occur. This is in contrast to the *Homo Economicus* (H.E.) from the classical economic theory. The H.E. thinks rationally (*i.e.* estimates all chances correctly) and acts in his own interest (*i.e.* is predictable).

88    *The Royal Society of London* (www.royalsociety.org) is one of the oldest (1660) and most prestigious academies of sciences in the world. Martin Rees was also Master of Trinity College, University of Cambridge (U.K.) from 2004 until 2012, where he held the Chair of Sir Isaac Newton. Newton was a Fellow of Trinity College from 1661 to 1696 and likewise President of the Royal Society from 1703 until his death in 1727. On the occasion of the 350th anniversary of the Royal Society in 2010, a wonderful book was published by Bill Bryson: *Seeing Further – The Story of Science & The Royal Society*. The homologous societies in Belgium are the two Royal Academies of Belgium for Science and the Arts, dating back to 1772 (www.rasab.be), while in France is it the *Académie des sciences* established in 1666 and now part of the *Institut de France*.

89    All the internet links in Table 7 were accessed on 30 April 2015.

90    www.oecd.org/general/themarshallplanspeechatharvarduniversity5june1947.htm (Accessed 21 December 2015).

91    http://espas.eu/orbis/sites/default/files/generated/document/en/espas-report-2015_0.pdf (Accessed 20 December 2015).

92    https://www.gov.uk/government/collections/foresight-projects (Accessed 22 December 2015).

93    https://www.gov.uk/government/publications/global-strategic-trends-out-to-2045 (Accessed 22 December 2015).

94    The official Dutch name is *Wetenschappelijke Raad voor het Regeringsbeleid* – W.R.R.

95    The *Oxford Martin School* was founded in 2005 as the *James Martin Institute for Science and Innovation* (InSIS), headed by Steve Rayner and housed in the Saïd Business School. In 2007, InSIS expanded to 16 research centres and was renamed as the *James Martin 21st Century School*. The school took its current name as of 1 October 2010 – www.oxfordmartin.ox.ac.uk

96    https://www.sbs.ox.ac.uk/community/global-community/links-international-colleagues/oxford-futures-forum-0 (Accessed 21 December 2015).

97    http://reports.weforum.org/global-strategic-foresight-community (Accessed 22 December 2015).

98    Different translations are possible: *"Dare to be wise"– "Have the courage to use your wits"– "Dare to think"*. Originally attributed to Horace (Quintus Horatius Flaccus, 65 BC-8 BC) in his work *Epistularum Liber Primus*, but primarily known since Immanuel Kant used it in his influential 1784 book *What is enlightenment?* (Was ist Aufklärung?).

99    In the 17th century, swans were believed to exist only as white-feathered birds. Reports

of explorers in 1697 in Western Australia on swans that were coloured black, were initially ridiculed.

100  For an overview of the academic literature on the concept of sensemaking in organizations, see Tindemans B. (2006) *Corporate Entrepreneurship: The Role of Organizational Learning*, Cranfield University, School of Management, Cranfield, U.K.

# References

**A**

Abella, A. (2008). *Soldiers of Reason: the RAND Corporation and the rise of the American empire.* New York: Harcourt.

Acemoglu, D. & Robinson, J. (2012). *Why Nations Fail: the origins of power, prosperity and poverty.* London: Profile Books.

Aligica, P.D. & Weinstein, K.R. (Eds.) (2009). *The Essential Herman Kahn in defense of thinking.* Lanham, U.S.: Lexington Book.

Ariëns, H. & Van Genugten, L. (17 April 2015). Interview in Dutch with Adam Kahane, *IS Online.* www.oneworld.nl/lezen/interview/interview-met-adam-kahane (Accessed 20 December 2015).

**B**

Bayes, T. & Price, R. (1763). An essay towards solving a problem in the doctrine of chances. *Philosophical Transactions* 53, 370-418. http://rstl.royalsocietypublishing.org/content/53/370.full.pdf (Accessed 20 December 2015).

Babüroğlu, Oğuz N. (1988). The vortical environment: The fifth in the Emery-Trist levels of organizational environments. *Human Relations* 41 (3), 181-210.

Berger, G. (1957). Sciences humaines et prévisions. *Revue des Deux Mondes,* 3 (February), 417-426. www.laprospective.fr/dyn/francais/memoire/texte_fondamentaux/sciences-humaines-et-prevision-g-berger-1959.pdf (Accessed 20 December 2015).

Berger, G. (1964). *Étapes de la Prospective.* Paris : Presses Universitaires de France.

Berger, G., de Bourbon-Busset, J. & Massé, P. (2007). *De la Prospective: textes fondamentaux de la prospective française 1955-1966.* Paris: L'Harmattan.

Bertalanffy, L. von (1950). The theory of open systems in physics and biology. *Science,* 111, 23-29. www.markd.nl/content/references/1950Bertalanffy.pdf (Accessed 20 December 2015).

Bertalanffy, L. von (1969). *General System Theory.* New York: George Braziller Inc.

Bradfield, R., Wright, G., Burt, G., Cairns, G. & Van der Heijden, K. (2005). The origins and evolution of scenario techniques in long range business planning. *Futures,* 37 (8), 795-812.

Brier, G.W. (1950). Verification of Forecasts Expressed in Terms of Probability. *Monthly Weather Review,* 78, 13-3. http://docs.lib.noaa.gov/rescue/mwr/078/mwr-078-01-0001.pdf (Accessed 5 January 2016).

Bryson, B. (Ed.) (2010). *Seeing Further: the story of science & The Royal Society.* London: HarperPress.

Burt, G., Van der Heijden, K. (2003). First steps: towards purposeful activities in scenario thinking and future studies. *Futures,* 35 (10), 1011-1026.

## C

Cairns, G., Wright, G., Bradfield, R., Van der Heijden, K. & Burt, G. (2004). Exploring e-government futures through the application of scenario planning. *Technological forecasting and social change*, 71(3), 217-238.

Cairns, G., Wright, G., van der Heijden, K., Bradfield, R. & Burt, G. (2006). Enhancing foresight between multiple agencies: issues in the use of scenario thinking to overcome fragmentation, *Journal of Futures*, 38 (8), 1010-1025.

Carter, T.R., Jones, R.N., Lu, X., Bhadwal, S., Conde, C., Mearns, L.O., O'Neill, B.C., Rounsevell, M.D.A. &Zurek, M.B. (2007). New assessment methods and the characterisation of future conditions. In: Parry, M.L., Canziani, O.F., Palutikof, J.P., Van der Linden, P.J., Hanson, C.E. (Eds.), *Climate Change 2007: impacts, adaptation and vulnerability. Contribution of working group II to the fourth assessment report of the Intergovernmental Panel on Climate Change* (pp. 133-171). Cambridge: Cambridge University Press.

Churchill, W.S. (1946). The Sinews of Peace. In: Kishlansky, M.A. (Ed.) (1995). *Sources of World History*, (298-302). New York: Harper Collins. http://en.wikisource.org/wiki/Sinews_of_Peace (Accessed 20 December 2015).

Chesbrough, H. (2006). *Open Innovation: the new imperative for creating and profiting from technology*. Boston: Harvard Business School Press.

Clark, G. (2007). *A Farewell to Alms: A brief economic history of the world*. Princeton, New Jersey: Princeton University Press.

Clausewitz, C. von (1982). *On War*. London: Penguin Books.

Collier, P. (2010). *The Plundered Planet*. New York: Oxford University Press.

Coates, J., Durance, P. & Godet, M. (2010). Special issue: strategic foresight. *Technological forecasting and social change*, 77 (9), 1423-1599.

## D

Daft, R.L. & Wieck, K.E. (1984). Toward a model of organizations as interpretation systems. *Academy of Management Review*, 9 (2), 284-295.

Dalkey, N. & Helmer, O. (1963). An experimental application of the Delphi method to the use of experts. *Management Science*, 9 (3), 458-467.

Day, G.S. & Schoemaker, P.J.H. (2004a). Peripheral vision: sensing and acting on weak signals. *Long Range Planning*, 37 (2), 117-121.

Day, G.S. & Schoemaker, P.J.H. (2004b). Driving through the fog: managing at the edge, *Long Range Planning*, 37 (2), 127-143.

Day, G.S. & Schoemaker, P.J.H. (2005). Scanning the periphery, *Harvard Business Review*, 83 (11), 135-148.

De Brabandere, L. (2005). *The Forgotten Half of Change: achieving greater creativity through changes in perception*. Chicago: Dearborn Trade Publishing.

De Geus, A.P. (1992). Modelling to predict or to learn? *European Journal of Operations Research*, 59 (1), 1-5.

De Geus, A. (1997). *The Living Company: habits for survival in a turbulent environment*. Boston: Harvard Business School Press.

Diamond, J.M. (1997). *Guns, Germs and Steel: the fates of human societies*. New York: W.W. Norton & Co.

Dickson, P.R., Farris, P.W. & Verbeke, W.J.M.I. (2001). Dynamic strategic thinking. *Journal of the Academy of Marketing Science*, 29 (3), 216-237.

Dylan E. (2012). *Risk Intelligence: how to live with uncertainty*. New York: Free Press.


**E**

Eden, C. & Ackermann, F. (2000). Mapping distinctive competencies: a systemic approach. *Journal of the operational Research Society*, 51 (1), 12-20.

Einstein, A. (1948). A Message to Intellectuals. In: Green J. (Ed.) (2003) *Albert Einstein*. Melbourne/New York: Ocean Press. (p. 52).

Emery, F.E. & Trist, E. (1965). The causal texture of organization environments. *Human Relations*, 18 (1), 21-32. http://hum.sagepub.com/content/18/1/21.full.pdf (Accessed 20 December 2015).

Emery, F.E. & Trist, E. (1972). *Towards a Social Ecology: contextual appreciation of the future in the present*. London: Plenum.

Emery, F.E. (1977). *Futures we are in*. Leiden: Martinus Nijhoff.

Etzkowitz, H. & Ranga, M. (2009). A trans-Keynesian vision of innovation for the contemporary economic crisis: 'picking winners' revisited. *Science and Public Policy*, 36 (10), 799-808.


**F**

Fahey, L. & Randall, R. (1998). *Learning from the Future: competitive foresight scenario*. New York: John Wiley & Sons.

Fassin, Y. & Gosselin, D. (2011). The collapse of a European bank in the financial crisis: an analysis from stakeholder and ethical perspectives. *Journal of Business Ethics*, 102 (2), 169-191.

Ferguson, N. (2011). *Civilization: the West and the Rest*. London: Allen Lane (Penguin Books).

Ferro, M. (2015). *L'Aveuglment: Une autre histoire de notre monde*. Paris: Tallandier.

Fukuyama, F. (1989). The End of History. *The National Interest*, 16 (Summer), 3-18. www.kropfpolisci.com/exceptionalism.fukuyama.pdf (Accessed 20 December 2015).

Fukuyama, F. (1992). *The End of History and The Last Man*. New York: Free Press.


**G**

Gaudin, T. (2005). *La Prospective*. Paris: Presses Universitaires de France.

Georghiou, L., Cassingena, J., Keenan, M., Miles, I. & Popper, R. (Eds.) (2008). *The Handbook of Technology Foresight*. Cheltenham, UK: Edward Elgar.

Gharajedaghi, J. (2011). *Systems Thinking: managing chaos and complexity*. Burlington, MA, U.S.: Morgan Kaufmann.

Glenn, J.C. & Gordon T.J. (Eds.) (2009). *Futures Research Methodology*, version 3.0 (CD-ROM). Washington DC: The Millennium Project, American Council of the UN University. www.millennium-project.org/millennium/FRM-V3.html (Accessed 20 December 2015).

Godet, M. (1986). Introduction to la prospective: seven key ideas and one scenario method. *Futures*, 18 (2), 134-157.

Godet, M. (1990). Integration of scenarios and strategic management: using relevant, consistent and likely scenarios. *Futures*, 22 (7), 730-739.

Godet, M. (2000). The art of scenarios and strategic planning: tools and pitfalls. *Technological Forecasting and Social Change*, 65 (1), 3-22.

Goodwin, P. & Wright, G. (2001). Enhancing strategy evaluation in scenario planning: a role for decision analysis. *Journal of Management Studies*, 38 (1), 1-16.

Gordon, T.J. (2009). Cross-impact Method. In: Glenn, J.C. & Gordon, T.J. (Eds.), *Futures Research Methodology*. Washington DC: The Millennium Project, American Council of the UN University.

Gore, A. (2013). *The Future: Six Drivers of Global Change*. New-York: Random House.

Gosselin, D.P. (1986). Delphi-methodologie: technieken en koncepten voor strategische voorspellingen. *Het Ingenieursblad*, 55 (4), 181-187.

Gosselin, D. (1987). Evolution of computer integrated manufacturing in Flanders 1985-1995, a Delphi survey. *Journal A*, 28 (2), 91-94.

Gosselin, D.P. (2002). *Strategisch Accountmanagement: account-management vanuit een strategisch perspectief*. Gent: Universiteit Gent.

Gosselin, D.P. & Leysen, J. (2008). Vision of evolutions in the petroleum market. *European Review of Energy Markets*, 2 (3), 131-163.

Gosselin, D.P. & Huerre, T. (2010). À quoi pourraient ressembler les 2030´s et les au-delà? In: Duclos, P. & Tribot la Spière, L. (Eds.), *L'Europe sous tension énergétique*. Paris: Centre d'Étude et de Prospective Stratégique (CEPS).

Gosselin, D. & Tindemans, B. (2011). *Traceurs d'Avenir: l'art d'anticiper l'imprévisible*. Bruxelles: Éditions Racine.

Gosselin, D. (2012). Blinde vlekken en black outs van onze energiepolitiek. *De Morgen*, 15 May 2012, p. 21. www.demorgen.be/dm/nl/2461/DeGedachte/article/detail/1438679/2012/05/15/Blinde-vlekken-en-black-outs-van-onze-energiepolitiek.dhtml (Accessed 20 December 2015).

Gosselin, D.P., et. al. (2013). *Perspectives on a Hyperconnected World: Insights from the Science of Complexity*, Global Agenda Council on Complex Systems, World Economic Forum. http://www3.weforum.org/docs/WEF _GAC_ PerspectivesHyperconnectedWorld_ExecutiveSummary_2013.pdf (Accessed 18 August 2015).

Grint, K. (2008). Leadership 1965-2006: Forward to the past or back to the future? In: Dopson, S., Earl, M. & Snow, P. (Eds.), *Mapping the Management Journey*. Oxford: Oxford University Press.


**H**

Hamel, G & Prahalad, C.K. (1989). Strategic Intent. *Harvard Business Review*, 67 (3), 63-78.

Hesse, H. (1922). *Siddhartha*. (1st English ed. 1951). New York: New Directions. www.gutenberg.org/files/2500/2500-h/2500-h.htm (Accessed 20 December 2016).

Helmer, O. & Rescher, N. (1959). On the Epistemology of the Inexact Sciences. *Management Science*, 6 (1), 25-52.

Heuer, R.J. (1999). *Psychology of Intelligence Analysis* (chapter 8: Analysis of Competing Hypotheses). Washington DC: Center for the Study of Intelligence, Central Intelligence Agency. https://www.cia.gov/library/center-for-the-study-of-intelligence/csi-publications/books-and-monographs/psychology-of-intelligence-analysis/PsychofIntelNew.pdf (Accessed 20 December 2015).

Hughes, N. (2009). *A historical overview of strategic scenario planning.* Ref UKERC/WP/ESM/2009/011.UK: UK Energy Research Centre. www.lowcarbonpathways.org.uk/lowcarbon/publications/Hughes_x2009x_UKERC_Scenarios_WP1_-_web.pdf (Accessed 20 December 2015).

## I

Ingvar, David H. (1985). Memories of the future: an essay on the temporal organization of conscious awareness. *Human Neurobiology*, 4 (3), 127-136.

## J

Jones, M. & Silberzahn, P. (2013). *Constructing Cassandra: Reframing Intelligence Failure at the CIA, 1947–2001.* Stanford: Stanford University Press.

Jouvenel, B. de (1948). *On Power: The Natural History of Its Growth.* Indianapolis, Indiana, U.S.: Liberty Fund.

Jouvenel, H. de (2000). A brief methodological guide to scenario building. *Technological Forecasting and Social Change*, 65 (1), 37-48.

## K

Kahane, A. (1992). The Mont Fleur scenarios: what will South Africa be like in the year 2002? *Deeper News*, 7 (1). Emeryville: Global Business Network.

Kahn, H. (1960). *On Thermonuclear War.* Princeton: Princeton University Press.

Kahn, H. (1965). *On Escalation,* New York: Praeger.

Kahn, H. (1979). The agnostic use of information and concepts. In: *World Economic Development: 1979 and beyond* (pp. 167-176). Boulder, U.S.: Westview Press.

Kahn, H. & Wiener, A. (1967). *The Year 2000: a framework for speculation on the next thirty-three years.* New York: Macmillan.

Kahneman, D. (2011). *Thinking Fast and Slow.* New York: Farrar, Straus and Giroux.

Kahneman, D. & Tversky, A. (1979). Prospect theory: an analysis of decision under Risk. *Econometrica*, 47 (2), 263-291. www.princeton.edu/~kahneman/docs/Publications/prospect_theory.pdf (Accessed 20 December 2015).

Kay, J. (2010). *Obliquity.* London: Profile Books.

Kent, S. (1964). *The Theory of Intelligence.* Langley, VA: CIA, Center for the Study of Intelligence. https://www.cia.gov/library/center-for-the-study-of-intelligence/csi-publications/books-and-monographs/sherman-kent-and-the-board-of-national-estimates-collected-essays/the-theory-of-intelligence.html (Accessed 5 January 2016).

Keough, S.M. & Shanahan, K.J. (2008). Scenario planning: towards a more complete model for practice. *Advances in Developing Human Resources*, 10 (2), 166-178.

Klayman, J. & Schoemaker, P.J.H. (1993). Thinking about the future: a cognitive perspective. *Journal of Forecasting*, 12 (2), 161-186.

Kleiner, A. (2003). *Who Really Matters: the core group theory of power, privilege and success.* New York: Doubleday Currency.

Knight, F.H. (1921). *Risk, Uncertainty, and Profit.* Boston, MA: Houghton & Mifflin.

Knowledge@Wharton (22 July 2009): interview met Gosselin D.P.: *Eyes Wide Open: embracing uncertainty through scenario planning.* http://knowledge.wharton.upenn. edu/article.cfm?articleid=2298 (Accessed 20 December 2015).

Korte, R.F. & Chermack, T.J. (2007). Changing organizational culture with scenario planning. *Futures,* 39 (6), 645-656.


**L**

Lang, T. (2008). Systemizing the organizational scenario literature using Morgan's metaphors. In: Solomon, G. (Ed.), *Proceedings of the sixty-seventh annual meeting of the Academy of Management.* U.S.: Academy of Management.

Le Roux, P., *et al.* (1992). The Mont Fleur Scenarios. *Deeper News* 7 (1). Emeryville: Global Business Network.

Lesourne, J. & Stoffaës, C. (1996). *La Prospective Stratégique d'Entreprise.* Paris: Inter Editions.

Lim, Y.K. & Sato, K. (2006). Describing multiple aspects of use situation: applications of design information framework (DIF) to scenario development. *Design Studies,* 27 (1), 57-76.

Linstone, H.A. & Turoff, M. (Eds.) (1975). *The Delphi Method: techniques and applications.* Reading, MA: Addison-Wesley Pub. Co. http://is.njit.edu/pubs/delphibook/ delphibook.pdf (Accessed 20 December 2015).

Lumpkin, G.T. & Dess, G.G. (1996). Clarifying the entrepreneurial orientation construct and linking it to performance. *Academy of Management Review,* 21 (1), 135-172.


**M**

Massé, P. (1967). *Prévision et Prospective.* Paris: Presses Universitaires de France.

McCann, J.E. & Selsky, J. (1984). Hyperturbulence and the emergence of type 5 environments. *Academy of Management Review,* 9 (3), 460-470.

McDonough, W. & Braungart, M. (2002). *Cradle to Cradle: remaking the way we make things.* San Francisco, CA, U.S.: North Point Press.

McGrath, R. G. & MacMillan, I. C. (1995). Discovery Driven Planning, *Harvard Business Review,* 73 (4), 44-54.

McGrath, R. G. & MacMillan, I. C. (2009). *Discovery Driven Growth: a breakthrough process to reduce risk and seize opportunity.* Boston, MA: Harvard Business Publishing.

Morris, I. (2010). *Why the West Rules – For Now: the patterns of history and what they reveal about the future.* New York: Farrar, Straus and Giroux.

Mulgan, G. (2009). *The Art of Public Strategy: mobilizing power and knowledge for the common good.* Oxford: Oxford University Press.


**N**

Neumann, J. von & Morgenstern, O. (1944). *Theory of Games and Economic Behavior.* Princeton: Princeton University Press.

Nisbett, R. (2003). *The Geography of Thought: How Asians and Westerners Think Differently... And Why.* New York: Free Press.

Nisbett, R. (2015). Cognition East and West: Fundamental Differences in Reasoning and Perception. In: Harrison, L. & Yasin, E. (Eds.), *Culture Matters in Russia and Everywhere: Backdrop of the Russia-Ukraine Conflict* (pp. 303-312). Lanham, U.S.: Lexington Book.

Normann, R. (2001). *Reframing Business.* Chichester, UK: John Wiley & Sons.


**O**

O'Brien, F. & Meadows, M. (2007). Developing a visioning methodology: visioning choices for the future of operational research. *Journal of the operational Research Society,* 58 (5), 557-575.

Orrell, D. (2007). *The Future of Everything.* New York: Thunder's Mouth Press.

Oxford Martin School, University of Oxford. (2013). *Now for the Long Term: The Report of the Oxford Martin Commission for Future Generations.* Oxford, U.K.: Oxford Martin School.

www.oxfordmartin.ox.ac.uk/downloads/commission/Oxford_Martin_Now_for_the_Long_Term.pdf (Accessed 20 December 2015).


**P**

Pachauri, R.K. & Reisinger, A. (Eds.) (2007). *Quatrième rapport d'évaluation du GIEC.* Genève, Suisse: GIEC.

Petersen, J. (1999). *Out of the Blue: how to anticipate big future surprises.* Lantham, Maryland: Madison Books.

Piketty, T. (2014). *Capital in the Twenty-First Century.* Boston, U.S.: Harvard University Press. [Original book published in French in (2013). *Le Capital au XXIe siècle.* Paris: Éditions du Seuil.]

Popper, R. (2008a). How are foresight methods selected? *Foresight,* 10 (6), 62–89.

Popper, R. (2008b). Foresight methodology. In: Georghiou, L., Cassingena, J., Keenan, M., Miles, I. & Popper, R. (Eds.), *The Handbook of Technology Foresight* (pp. 44-88). Cheltenham, UK: Edward Elgar.

Postma, T.J.B.M. & Liebl, F. (2005). How to improve scenario analysis as a strategic management tool? *Technological Forecasting and Social Change,* 72 (2), 161-173.

Prins, G. & Rayner, S. (Eds.) (2010). *The Hartwell Paper: A new direction for climate policy after the crash of 2009.* Institute for Science, Innovation and Society, Oxford Martin School, University of Oxford, UK. http://eureka.bodleian.ox.ac.uk/209/1/Hartwell.pdf (Accessed 20 December 2015).


**R**

Ramirez, R. (2008). Forty years of scenarios: retrospect and prospect. In: Dopson, S., Earl, M. & Snow, P. (Eds.), *Mapping the Management Journey,* 308-319. Oxford: Oxford University Press.

Ramirez, R. & Ravetz, J. (2011). Feral futures: Zen and Aesthetics. *Futures,* 43 (4), 478-487.

Ramirez, R., Selsky, J.W. & Van der Heijden, K. (2009). *Causal texture theories of turbulence and the growth and role of scenario practices*. In: The European Academy of Management (EURAM) Conference, May 2009, Liverpool, UK. http://sbs.eprints.org/id/eprint/3170 (Accessed 20 December 2015).

Ramirez, R., Selsky, J.W. & Van der Heijden, K. (Eds.) (2010). *Business Planning for Turbulent Times: new methods for applying scenarios*. (2nd Edition) London: Earthscan.

Ramirez, R., Van der Heijden, K. & Selsky, J. (2008). Conceptual and historical overview. In: Ramirez, R., Selsky, J. & Van der Heijden, K. (Eds.), *Business Planning for Turbulent Times: new methods for applying scenarios* (pp. 17-31). London: Earthscan.

Ramo, J.C. (2009). *The Age of The Unthinkable*. New York: Little, Brown and Company.

Raubitschek, R. (1988). Multiple scenario analysis and business planning. In: R. Lamb, P. Shrivastava (Eds.), *Advances in Strategic Management*, vol. 5. London: JAI Press Inc.

Rees, M.J. (2003). *Our Final Century*. London: William Heinemann.

Rittel, H.W.J. & Webber, M.M. (1973). Dilemmas in a general theory of planning. *Policy Sciences*, 4 (2), 155-169. www.uctc.net/mwebber/Rittel+Webber+Dilemmas+General_Theory_of_Planning.pdf (Accessed 14 December 2015).

Roquebert, J.A., Phillips, R.L. & Westfal, P.A. (1996). Market versus management: what drives profitability? *Strategic Management Journal*, 17 (8), 653-664.


**S**

Saïd Business School, University of Oxford. (2015). *The CEO Report: Embracing the Paradoxes of Leadership and the Power of Doubt*. Joint research report: Saïd Business School and Heidrick & Struggles. www.sbs.ox.ac.uk/sites/default/files/Press_Office/Docs/The-CEO-Report-Final.pdf (Accessed 20 December 2015).

Sanders, T.I. (1998). *Strategic Thinking and the New Science: Planning in the midst of chaos, complexity and change*. New York: The Free Press.

Scearce, D., Fulton, K. (2004). *What If? The Art of Scenario Thinking for Non-Profits*. Emeryville: Global Business Network. www.monitorinstitute.com/downloads/what-we-think/what-if/What_If.pdf (Accessed 20 December 2015).

Schoemaker, P.J.H. (1991). When and how to use scenario planning: a heuristic approach with illustration. *Journal of Forecasting*, 10 (6), 549-564.

Schoemaker, P.J.H. (1992). How to link strategic vision to core capabilities. *Sloan Management Review*, 34 (1), 67-81.

Schoemaker, P.J.H. (1993a). Multiple scenario development: its conceptual and behavioral foundation. *Strategic Management Journal*, 14 (3), 193-213.

Schoemaker, P.J.H. (1993b). Determinants of risk-taking behavioral and economic views. *Journal of Risk and Uncertainty*, 6 (1), 49-73.

Schoemaker, P.J.H. (1995). Scenario planning: a tool for strategic thinking. *Sloan Management Review*, 36 (2), 25-40.

Schoemaker, P.J.H. (1997). Disciplined imagination. *International Studies of Management & Organization*, 27 (2), 43-70.

Schoemaker, P.J.H. & Schoemaker, J.A. (1995). Estimating environmental liability-quantifying the unknown. *California Management Review*, 37 (3), 29-61.

Schoemaker, P.J.H. & Gunther, R.E. (2006). The wisdom of deliberate mistakes. *Harvard Business Review*, 84 (6), 108-115.

Schön, D.A. (1983). *The Reflective Practitioner: how professionals think in action*. London: Temple Smith.

Schön, D.A. (1987). *Educating the Reflective Practitioner*. San Francisco: Jossey Bass.

Schwartz, P. (1996). *The Art of the Long View: paths to strategic insight for yourself and your company*. (2nd Ed.) New York: Doubleday Currency.

Schwarz, J.O. (2008). Assessing the future of futures studies in management. *Futures*, 40 (3), 237-246.

Senge, P. (1990). *The Fifth Discipline*. New York: Doubleday Currency.

Senge, P., Kleiner, A., Roberts, C., Ross, R., Roth, G. & Smith, B. (1999a). *The Dance of Change: the challenges to sustaining momentum in learning organizations*. New York: Doubleday Currency.

Senge, P., Kleiner, A., Roberts, C., Ross, R., Roth, G. & Smith, B. (1999b). *The Fifth Discipline Fieldbook: strategies and tools for building a learning organization*. New York: Doubleday Currency.

Shell International (2003). *Exploring the Future, Scenario's: an explorer's guide*. London: Shell Centre.


**T**

Taleb, N.N. (2007). *The Black Swan: the impact of the highly improbable*. New York: Random House.

Tetlock, P.E. (2005). *Expert Political Judgment: how good is it? How can we know?* Princeton: Princeton University Press.

Tetlock, P.E. & Gardner D. (2015). *Superforecasting: The Art and Science of Prediction*. New York: Crown Publishers.

Tindemans, B. (2006). *Corporate Entrepreneurship: the role of organizational learning*. Cranfield, UK: Cranfield University, School of Management.

Teulings, C. & Baldwin, R., (Eds.) (2014) *Secular Stagnation: Facts, Causes, and Cures*. London: Centre for Economic Policy Research (CEPR). www.voxeu.org/sites/default/files/Vox_secular_stagnation.pdf (Accessed 20 December 2015).

Tuchman, B. W. (1984). *The March of Folly: From Troy to Vietnam*. New York: Alfred A. Knopf (currently Random House).


**V**

Van Asselt, M.B.A., Faas, A., Van der Molen, F. & Veenman, S.A., (Eds.) (2010). *Out of Sight: exploring futures for policymaking*. Amsterdam: Amsterdam University Press. www.wrr.nl/fileadmin/en/publicaties/PDF-samenvattingen/Exploring_Futures_for_Policymaking.pdf (Accessed 16 December 2015).

Van Asselt, M.B.A., Van 't Klooster, S.A., Van Notten, P.W.F. & Smits, L.A. (2010). *Foresight in Action: developing policy-oriented scenarios*. London: Earthscan.

Van der Heijden, K. (2000). Scenarios and forecasting: two perspectives. *Technological Forecasting and Social Change*, 65 (1), 31-36.

Van der Heijden, K. (2004). Can internally generated futures accelerate organizational learning? *Journal of Futures*, 36 (2), 145-159.

Van der Heijden, K. (2005). *Scenarios: the art of strategic conversation.* (2nd Ed.) Chichester: John Wiley & Sons. www.laprospective.fr/dyn/francais/memoire/texte_fondamentaux/the-art-of-strategic-conversation-van-der-heijden.pdf (Accessed 20 December 2015).

Van der Heijden, K., Bradfield, R., Burt, G., Cairns, G. & Wright, G. (2002). *The Sixth Sense: accelerating organizational learning with scenarios.* Chichester: John Wiley and Sons.

Van der Merwe, L., (2008). Scenario-based strategy in practice: a framework. *Advances in Developing Human Resources*, 10 (2), 216-239.

Van Notten, P., Sleegers, A.M. & Van Asselt, M. (2005). The future shocks: on discontinuity and scenario development. *Technological Forecasting and Social Change*, 72 (2), 175-94.

Van'tKlooster, S.A. & Van Asselt, M.B.A. (2006). Practicing the scenario-axes technique. *Futures*, 38 (1), 15-30.

**W**

Wack, P. (1985a). Scenarios: uncharted waters ahead. *Harvard Business Review*, 63 (5), 72-89.

Wack, P. (1985b). Scenarios: shooting the rapids. *Harvard Business Review*, 63 (6), 139-150.

Wagner, C. (2004). Enterprise strategy management systems: current and next generation. *Journal of Strategic information Systems*, 13 (2), 105-128.

Weber, K. & Glynn, M. (2006). Making sense with institutions: context, thought and action in Karl Weick's theory. *Organization Studies*, 27 (11), 1639-1660.

Weick, K. (1988). Enacted sensemaking in crisis situations. *Journal of Management Studies*, 25 (4), 305-317.

Weick, K. (1995). *Sensemaking in Organisations.* London: Sage.

Weick, K., Sutcliffe, K. & Obstfeld, D. (2005). Organizing and the process of sensemaking. *Organization Science*, 16 (4), 409-421.

Wittgenstein, L. J. (1922). *TractatusLogico-Philosophicus.* London: Keagan Paul, Trench, Trubner. www.gutenberg.org/files/5740/5740-pdf.pdf (Accessed 20 December 2015).

Wilkinson, A. (2009). Scenarios Practices: In Search of Theory. *Journal Future Studies*, 13(3), 107-114. www.jfs.tku.edu.tw/13-3/S06.pdf (Accessed 20 December 2015).

Williams, D. (2009). *Trevor Manuel: "I could close my eyes now…".*Online source: http://connecteddale.com/trevor-manuel-i-could-close-my-eyes-now (Accessed 20 December 2015).

Wright, G., Van der Heijden, K., Burt, G., Bradfield, R. & Cairns, G. (2007). Scenario planning interventions in organizations: an analysis of the causes of success and failure. *Journal of Futures*, 40 (3), 218-236.

# Index